Medicine Balls

Medicine Balls

Dr Phil Hammond

BLACK & WHITE PUBLISHING

First published 2007
by Black & White Publishing Ltd
99 Giles Street, Edinburgh EH6 6BZ

3 5 7 9 10 8 6 4   08 09 10 11

ISBN 13:   978 1 84502 188 7
ISBN 10:   1 84502 188 6

Typeset by RefineCatch Limited, Bungay, Suffolk
Printed and bound by MPG Books Ltd Bodmin, Cornwall

Dr Rose is lovely

CONTENTS

CONTENTS

INTRODUCTION

The KitKat is three layers of cream-filled wafer covered in an outer layer of chocolate. This qualifies it to appear on both biscuit and chocolate shelves of the supermarket, thus doubling its exposure and sales.

Medicine Balls is a semi-autobiographical medico-political self-help comedy novel with poems. Please let me know in which section of the store you found it – biscuits or chocolate.

Satirising the NHS is a lot easier than working in it but I still do as much doctoring as the GMC allows because it's interesting and I need the material. Comedy has always been my therapy but what started as self-indulgent catharsis has, I hope, morphed into something more constructive over the years. I'm still passionate about the ideals of the NHS and much of this book is dedicated to saving them. At least until I'm a patient.

I've written for *Private Eye* almost for as long as I've worked in the NHS. It's the closest thing we have to a free press and it's fiercely anti-hypocrisy, which worries me slightly. As a doctor, do I practise what I preach? As a campaigner, do I make ridiculous suggestions for reforming the NHS that I ignore in the privacy of the consulting room?

Other themes are based around questions that keep me awake at night, for example:

- Why are doctors so miserable?
- Why is homeopathy so popular?
- Why did Lord Winston advertise omega-3-enriched clever milk?

- What's wrong with that bloke with the flaky skin who picked it off in front of me and left it on my desk?
- Does putting old ladies on twenty tablets a day make them healthier?
- What is health anyway?
- Is Gillian McKeith alive?
- Is Dr Rose asleep?
- Do you think she'll wake up if I do this very slowly?

Here's what else you could spend your £9.99 on:

- 1 tablet of Viagra
- 10 tablets of online fake Viagra
- 1,000 of Dr Phil's Magical Healing Love Tablets (contain no active ingredients whatsoever but work for a surprising variety of ailments)

It's your body. You decide.

Phil Hammond
drphil@bbc.co.uk
www.drphil2.com

PS Anything likely to get me struck off is fabricated. The rest is possibly true.

NIGEL

'Morning, Dr Hammond. What do you make of this then?'

'Very nice – Topshop?'

'Not the shirt – this.'

'How long have you had it?'

'A while. It started as one big patch and then spread into lots of little ones.'

'Just on your trunk?'

'Mainly. I've got a few at the top of my arms.'

'Oh, hang on. I know this one. It's psit something . . . psit, psit, psit . . . Bugger, it's gone. I'll just see what the computer says.'

'Google?'

'No, Patient UK. "Comprehensive, free, up-to-date health information as provided by GPs to patients during consultations." Psit, psit . . . psittacosis.'

'Isn't that what you get from parrots?'

'Have you got a parrot?'

'No.'

'Can't be that then.'

'It's pityriasis.'

'That's it. How do you know?'

'I've already looked it up.'

'How would you be spelling it?'

'P-I-T-Y-R-I-A-S-I-S.'

'Here we are. Pityriasis rosea. I'll just print off a patient information leaflet.'

'Are you here all week?'

'Just Thursdays.'

'Do you know much about skin?'

'"Pityriasis rosea is a rash thought to be caused by a virus. Although it can be quite dramatic, the illness is very mild. It commonly affects young adults but can affect all ages. It goes away on its own without any treatment." You can take that away if you like.'

'I've already got it.'

'What, this exact same leaflet?'

'Yes, it's easy to find.'

'So why have you come to see me?'

'I was thinking that. Why have I gone through the hassle of getting an appointment and taking time off work to hear you parrot a leaflet that I already have?'

'And the answer is?'

'You're the doctor. I thought you could confirm the diagnosis and add a bit extra.'

'Well, I can confirm the diagnosis. Would you like it in Greek?'

'It's from Greek. *Pituron* is bran, hence the shedding of fine scales.'

'Oh, right.'

'So it's not pityriasis versicolor or guttate psoriasis?'

'Remind me of the difference?'

'Or a drug eruption?'

'Are you taking any drugs?'

'No.'

'Cross that one off then.'

'Erythema migrans or multiforme?'

'Common things being common, I reckon it's pityriasis rosea.'

'Not secondary syphilis?'

'I doubt it. Could you put your list away now, please?'

'Are my patches light pink with the scaling confined to the edges?'

'Let's have you over by the window.'

'Can anyone see in?'

'Put the curtain over your head. Yes. The lesions are light pink with the scaling confined to the edges.'

2

'So it might be guttate psoriasis?'

'Yes?'

'Wrong. It's more likely to be pityriasis.'

'I meant no.'

'You really do know nothing about skin.'

'If you burn it, put it under the cold tap for at least twenty minutes and cover it with cling film.'

'Everyone knows that. Is there any medical knowledge you have on any subject that I can't get more reliably from a reputable internet site?'

'Don't use cling film as a condom.'

'Why would anyone do that?'

'Poverty, desperation, experimentation – the usual.'

'What about fascinating insights on what it means to be sick and how to cope?'

'Never been ill. Sorry.'

'So what's the point of you?'

'I'm not sure. Shall we have a little forage in Dr Phil's secret drawer?'

'Your secret drawer?'

'All doctors have them. Third one down on the right. Here we go.'

'Is that vodka?'

'Never mind that. What do you think of this?'

'It's a signed photo of Carol Vorderman.'

'Touch it. It's yours.'

'Truly?'

'Madly, deeply.'

'Have you got Susie Dent in Dictionary Corner?'

'Here you go. A matching set. Bookends for a blue Monday.'

'What about Des? For the wife.'

'Sorry. Cancer patients only.'

'She has got a suspicious mole.'

'Go on then.'

GLORIA

'Hello. Have a seat. I don't think we've met?'

'Thank you. So this is where the famous Dr Phil works.'

'On Thursdays, yes. Why do you ask?'

'You only work Thursdays?'

'Yes.'

'I'm not sure I want a doctor who only works Thursdays.'

'I'm not sure I would either. Dr Rose is lovely.'

'Is she on TV?'

'Not yet.'

'Dr Raj works a lot harder than you do.'

'Are you one of his patients?'

'No. I was hoping to produce *Dr Raj's Brain Gym* but we couldn't get a buyer.'

'What a pity. So you work in TV and you've moved to Keynsham?'

'Don't be silly. Compton Dando, three days a week.'

'Gloria Maynard.'

'That's it.'

'So what can I do for you?'

'I'm making a show called *The World's Greatest TV Doctor.*'

'Very funny.'

'Commissioned for the autumn on Four. Would you like to take part?'

'Is Dr Raj in?'

'He'll do it if you do it. Lord Winston's up for it.'

'Anyone else?'

'Dr Hilary. Obviously. All the saddo *Street Doctors*. And the unfortunates who got tricked into *Embarrassing Illnesses*. Lots of scary women, skin stretched over ambition. Gillian McKeith . . .'

'Is she a proper doctor?'

'She's a major sponsor. We're co-funded by her Fast Formula Horny Goat Weed Complex.'

'Splendid. What's the global competition like?'

'*Oprah*'s Dr Phil's in.'

'There you are then. Waste of my time.'

'You're at the back of the field but you'll get the *Countdown* vote.'

'Is there a format?'

'Two rounds. We look at your media work and then we compare it to your doctoring. Do TV doctors practise what they preach or do they just sell out?'

'Do you want the answer now?'

'We'd need to record some consultations, with your patients' consent.'

'For broadcast?'

'No, we tried that for the pilot. General practice is unbelievably dull TV. So we transcribe the consultations, edit out the howlers and recreate them with celebrity patients.'

'Jesus.'

'If only he was available. A panel led by the President of the GMC will mark you for safety and hypocrisy. And the public vote for empathy, sex appeal and entertainment.'

'Do I get to wear a technicolour dream coat?'

'Only if you win. You're more of a performer than most. I saw *89 Minutes to Save the NHS*.'

'Where?'

'Spalding. Have you published it?'

'No.'

'How many books have you written?'

'Just the one. It's out of print. But I've got a thousand copies in the garage.'

'The other Dr Phil's written ten.'

'All different?'

'Different enough. In a no-nonsense, love smart, listen to your heart, family first, self matters, turn your life around sort of a way.'

'I can't compete with that. What's the prize?'

'A lifetime supply of Horny Goat Weed. And you'll front your own Channel 4 series.'

'To do what I like with?'

'The working title is *Make Me Gay*. We lock twelve hetero men in a lighthouse and see if we can turn one of them.'

'By strapping him to the light?'

'With hard-core rent porn and ladyboys, mainly. And possibly goat weed. You've worked in sexual health, haven't you?'

'Only on the male side.'

'Even better. You could give it some credibility. Make informed comments about the fluidity of human sexuality.'

'Are you sure Lord Winston's up for it?'

'He thinks it'll be a fascinating journey. And he wants to move on from St Ivel's omega-3-enriched clever milk.'

'Can I think about it?'

'Excellent. So that'll be thirty-six of you going to the UK heats.'

'Thirty-six?'

'I'll need a show reel and some examples of your early work.'

'I've got some very old comedy scripts. But they're not for broadcast.'

'I'd still like to read them. To map your journey. And you need to find a publisher for *89 Minutes to Save the NHS*. You can't go into this without a book deal or you'll look ridiculously lightweight.'

'Is there anything else I can do for you?'

'I'm auditioning in Burkina Faso next week, so I'll need some antimalarials.'

'It'll be a private prescription, I'm afraid.'

'Look, do you want to be the World's Greatest TV Doctor or not?'

BARRY

'Dr Hammond.'

'Hello.'

'I think I've got something wrong with my prostrate.'

'Prostate. There's no second "r". Why?'

'Why is there only one "r" in prostate?'

'Why do you think there's something wrong with it?'

'Because I'm peeing all the time.'

'Since when?'

'Since I started drinking more water.'

'Ah. What's the stream like?'

'I can still get it over the hedge.'

'It's not your prostate then. But you are a neighbour from hell.'

'Could it be diabetes?'

'Could be. But there isn't any sugar in it.'

'That was quick.'

'The receptionist checked it. She does weight, height, smoking and wee.'

'What do the nurses do?'

'Chronic diseases, vaccinations, contraception, cervical screening, quality control and same-day emergencies.'

'So what do you do?'

'Why are you drinking more water?'

'Well, everyone does, don't they? I was coming home on the train and I'd forgotten my book so I counted all the passengers carrying a bottle of water around. One in three. I thought, you can't fool that many people. We must be in the middle of a dehydration epidemic. Why has nobody warned me? So I bought two big bottles of 100 per cent naturally carbonated Highland spring water.'

'And did you pee a lot afterwards?'

'Yes.'

'I'm just as gullible. I like my wee to be dilute and colourless. There's no particular rationale for this, other than it doesn't smell too bad when I splash it all over the seat and I'm too lazy to wipe it up.'

'Maybe it's your prostate.'

'I think I picked up the habit of drinking too much water after advising parents to push the fluids with hot children. Heavy nappies good, dry nappies bad. Full clear stream good, dark yellow trickle bad.'

'Why are you telling me this?'

'Because it's so rare for me to be able to empathise with a patient. I'm fit, I'm happy, I've never been sick and rarely can I look a man in the eye and say "I know how you feel". Have you had gonorrhoea?'

'No.'

'What a pity. But we're both waterholics, mere pawns in the net of the bottled water industry.'

'I think you mean prawns. With an "r".'

'Does it comfort you to know your doctor is just as capable of irrational behaviour as you are?'

'Not really, no.'

'I've got a lucky chair. When I sit in it, Chelsea win.'

'Don't they usually win anyway?'

'And if I look upwards and outwards when Frank Lampard takes a penalty, he always scores.'

'You're starting to worry me now.'

'You started it. You know doctors tell you the smallest thing you should put in your ear is your elbow?'

'Yes.'

'I once let a beach magician in Goa put tiny stones in my ears and then had to pay him hundreds of rupees to fish them out again. And I've done that thing with the cotton bud.'

'Back on earth, how much water do I need to keep me healthy without getting up and down like a bladder-powered jack-in-the-box?'

'Two litres a day, preferably clean.'

'Bottled or tap?'

'Tap is fine. But anyone who says you can't taste the difference hasn't used the toilet on a Virgin Explorer.'

'So I should pee out two litres to keep me in balance?'

'No. You pee a litre and lose the rest in sweat and breath. But you don't need to drink two litres of water a day.'

'You just said I did.'

'I said you need two litres of water a day but it doesn't have to be water.'

'Eh?'

'Most food is full of water. A cucumber is 98 per cent water, fruit and fish up to 90 per cent and meat is at least a third water. Add in coffee, tea, beer, Vimto, Red Bull and smoothies, and you may not need much water water.'

'But I like drinking lots of water water.'

'Fine. But if you don't need it you'll just pee it out along with all the vitamins you're swallowing that you don't need.'

'Can you drink yourself to death?'

'Yes, it's called drowning. Some people binge-drink cold water to try to detoxify or reduce their appetite for food but that's all balls.'

'I thought dehydration could make you fail at school.'

'That's love. Rocky Sharpe and the Replays. 1979.'

'Label?'

'Chiswick. Their first UK hit was "Rama Lama Ding Dong", 1978. In a temperate climate, very few children get dehydrated enough to affect school work, unless they've got a hangover or it's a heatwave.'

'So how do I know when I need to drink?'

'You're not going to believe this. Thirst.'

ALI

'Hello. Have a seat.'

'I'm intrigued by this note in the waiting room.'

'It's a consent form.'

'For what?'

'For me to transcribe your consultation.'

'Who's going to read it?'

'I am, and a woman called Gloria. And it could be recreated for Channel 4 with an actor. But only with your consent.'

'Who'd be interested in my problems?'

'I'm sure they're fascinating but I'm the one being assessed.'

'An exam?'

'Sort of. The programme is looking at whether TV doctors practise what they preach. So it would help if you read my book, *89 Minutes to Save the NHS*. There are free copies in the waiting room.'

'The photocopies?'

'Yes. I've published it myself. I'm trying to encourage patients to be awkward rather than good. Stand up to doctors, don't just lie back and take it.'

'The receptionist says you only do a day a week.'

'Which one?'

'Thursdays. You should know.'

'Which receptionist?'

'The jaundiced one with the low-set ears.'

'Are you a doctor?'

'I'm a poet.'

'I've never had a poetic patient.'

'Do you ask your patients if they write poetry?'

'No.'

'Your list might be full of poets.'

'Possibly.'

'Lots of people write poems for personal fulfilment. You should try it.'

'Yes, all right. I'm Dr Hammond.'

'Ali.'

'Just Ali?'

'Like Bono.'

'You're an Africophile rock legend and a temporary resident?'

'I think I'll be here a while but I'm just trying out a few of the GP practices to see which one suits me best.'

'How are we doing?'

'I'm not sure I want a doctor who only works Thursdays.'

'I'm not sure I would either. Dr Rose is lovely.'

'What do you do the rest of the week?'

'Do you watch *Countdown*?'

'No.'

'Were you at the Beecham's Honey and Hot Lemon Over the Counter Remedy of the Year Awards at the Savoy?'

'No.'

'I'm a bullshitter. Doctor, husband, father, teacher, broadcaster, comic, columnist, activist, school governor, rugby coach, motivational speaker, demotivational speaker, devout atheist, big pharma flunkey, big ginger hypocrite, dog lover, bad lover and very bad trumpeter. I'd really like to be a novelist but I can only do narrative.'

'Doctors aren't normally this forthcoming.'

'Neither am I but Gloria says if I want to win, I have to be HOT – honest, open and trustworthy.'

'Win what?'

'It's a competition. Didn't I say?'

'No.'

'To find the World's Greatest TV Doctor.'

'I can smell the desperation. What's in it for me?'

'The right to refuse if you don't like where we end up. And twenty quid per consultation, if it's broadcast.'

'Cash?'

'Only if you promise to declare it.'

'Do I sign here?'

'Yes. And once again after the consultation, if you're happy. Don't you want to read the book first?'

'You've already told me how to behave.'

'So what can I do for you?'

'I demand to have my cholesterol checked.'

'Too boring.'

'OK. I believe I can fly.'

'Now you're just being silly.'

'Do I get the twenty pounds?'

'No.'

'Do I get to choose which actor plays me?'

'I've no idea.'

'Dervla Kirwan it is then.'

NOTE TO GLORIA

Gloria,

Here's a transcript of the show. It started as a Radio 4 series, *28 Minutes to Save the NHS*, expanding to *59 Minutes* for Edinburgh and *89 Minutes* for the tour. Same material, stretched twice as far. Just like the NHS.

David Spicer made the rants funnier and I nicked a few gags from other doctors. I've updated it and hope to have a publisher by the time you get back from Africa.

Phil

PS I've left the Malarone at reception, with the HRT.
PPS Boil it, cook it, peel it or forget it.

89 MINUTES TO SAVE THE NHS
Part One: Loosening the Limpet

Hi. Thank you all for turning out. Must be bloody hard to see a doctor in Spalding.

The National Health Service. Much praised around the world but never copied. Bit of a clue there. So who thinks the NHS is worth saving? . . . Almost all of you. Who thinks Labour has saved it? . . . Almost none of you.

Tony Blair famously said there were twenty-four hours to save the NHS, and that was just 89,276 hours ago. But then he was psychotic. I've written a poem to commemorate his gallant attempts at remodelling my world:

> Record investment, record debt
> Lots of targets, half not met
> Choose and bollocks, blame GPs
> Six hundred thousand dead Iraqis.

Mind the Gap
I did vote Labour back in 1997 because I thought the gap between rich and poor might narrow. But it's got wider. We've now have mass involuntary euthanasia in the UK. It's called living in the north. A boy born in Dorset will live on average ten years longer than a boy born in Manchester or Glasgow.

Within cities there are huge differences. If you leave Westminster on the Jubilee line going east, you lose a year of life expectancy for each station you get to. Percentage wise, there's more TB in Tower Hamlets than sub-Saharan Africa. And that's not Tony Blair. Whoever he was.

There are also chasms in health behaviour over small distances. I live just outside Bristol in Britain's greenest village, which means we recycle our bottle tops to assuage the guilt of doing the school run in a Mitsubishi Land Destroyer. We're only six miles from Knowle West but culturally we might as well be on another planet.

We hired a magician for my daughter's birthday party who did these amazing balloon sculptures, climaxing with the National Lottery Thunderball Draw – one big sausage balloon full of lots of little round balloons. Great for Knowle West but completely lost on an audience of prim, middle-class girls. The magician got a bit ratty and shouted, 'C'mon – what do your parents do on a Saturday afternoon? The National . . . The National . . . The National . . .'

A girl put her hand up and said, 'Trust?'

Politicians believe that the way to narrow the health gap is to heckle the poor into living well. Does it work? If you've got no job, no house, no garden, no self-esteem, no future and no reason to live, you're unlikely to pop down to Waitrose for a couple of oily fish and a punnet of sundried tomatoes. If you're living in a cardboard box under a bridge, you may not examine your testicles once a month. Mind you, if you live in a cardboard box, that's all you do. But people need hope before they'll even think about health.

As well as creating one of the most unequal societies in Europe, Labour has given us one of the most unequal health services. The NHS is very different in England, Scotland, Wales and Northern Ireland. You go to England for quick operations, Wales for free prescriptions, Scotland for elderly care and Northern Ireland if you hate change.

And within each country there are huge differences in health care, depending on whether your GP is alive and if your hospital has any specialists or money left. Say you've got a few months to live and want to try a new drug to buy a few more.

Some areas pay for wonderfully expensive drugs before NICE tells them they can, some allow you to top up your NHS care with private prescriptions, some make you remortgage the house and go private for everything. After ten years of Labour, there are still huge inequalities in services from IVF to dementia depending on where you live. So what does Gordon Brown do to tackle this postcode lottery? Appoints a postman as Health Secretary. Genius.

Sex and Dementia

Talking of lotteries, who's had a sexually transmitted infection? Hands up . . . Only me? Ten per cent of you have got chlamydia. I can smell it. Actually, chlamydia often has no symptoms which is why 10 per cent of you don't know you've got it. But ladies can do their own swabs these days. And no more umbrellas down the knob for men. You just have to pee in a pot. If you look under your seat, you'll find Dr Phil's discreetly packaged screening kit.

Don't be alarmed. I spent eighteen months working in a sexual health centre, or clap clinic as we used to call it. There are two great perks. One, you do occasionally see a man with an even smaller knob than you've got. 'YES!!!!' . . . would be an entirely inappropriate response in the circumstances. Two, you get to ask the kind of questions that in any other context would get you a smack in the mouth. 'Was it oral, vaginal or anal, vicar? OK, animal, mineral or vegetable?'

It takes a lot to get a man into the clinic. He'll happily go round the back of the chippie for a knee-trembler, no condom. Give it a few days and he's pissing razor blades. Dripping with pus. Just an observation.

'I know what to do. I'll treat myself.'

First up it's shower gel down the hole, then maybe Domestos. Followed by a pipe cleaner.

'You've been a naughty boy.'

And the best treatment for genital warts is not a cheese grater. Trust me.

Finally, when the whole package has swollen up beyond recognition, he'll come to the clinic.

'What have you done that for?'

'So my wife won't know I've been unfaithful.'

'I think she might suspect. You've got bollocks like a pair of spacehoppers.'

'At least they're bigger than yours, doctor.'

'Indeed they are . . . vicar.'

One reason people avoid clap clinics is embarrassment and shame; another is they're not great places to be. The clinic where I worked is a box on top of a plague pit. My room had no windows. On a hot day it smelt like the winners' tent at Frome Cheese Festival.

But no one marches on the streets for a breezier clap clinic, no one writes to *The Times* about the waiting list for warts. To save the NHS, we need fair treatment for illnesses that don't get a front-page splash. To get noticed, you need celebrity endorsement and there's a strict pecking order. Madonna's got breast cancer, Camilla's got osteoporosis, can you guess what I've got? Yep, herpes. I'm a patron of the Herpes Viruses Association. We don't have much money so I've designed my own ribbon. If you look closely, you'll see these cute little blisters.

Herpes causes more psychological damage than physical but it's a similar virus to chickenpox and no one worries about that. Think of herpes as chickenpox on your knob. Or a cold sore gone south. No picnic but drug companies have turned up the scare to sell more pills.

Then there's epilepsy. One in five patients with epilepsy is misdiagnosed or mistreated. There are more epilepsy specialists in the average American city than there are in the UK. So where are the celebs shouting, 'I have seizures!'?

Dementia. Hugely neglected. If we throw all our money at heart disease and cancer, we're all going to end up penniless. Either with dementia, caring for someone with dementia or trying to find a home for Mother. We're not even inching towards taking it seriously. It needs a new Thora Hird going up and down on a stairlift, singing 'Somewhere over the Rainbow'.

Depression. The biggest health threat of the twenty-first century. It gets you when you're young and, if you don't kill yourself, it stalks you for life. But we don't talk about it. Who's been on a 'glad to be mad' march?

Obesity, as big a killer as smoking. No one loves a fat celebrity, so there aren't any. Research found that American female college graduates would rather date a rapist or a murderer than an obese man. What's a fat boy gotta do to get laid?

So let's have ribbons for every disease: that'll save the NHS. Are you with me?

Trust Me, I'm a Love Tablet
Two other things that can save the NHS. The first is my bestselling book, *Trust Me, I'm a Doctor*. There are only a thousand in existence, all in a bag backstage. When I wrote it, I believed that the way to save the NHS was to encourage people to be far more sceptical about health care, to stand up to doctors and ask awkward, challenging questions. Trouble is, you get awkward, challenging answers. Once you've realised that doctors aren't nearly as powerful as you'd hoped and drugs don't work half as well, you can't put the genie back. You've burst the bubble of blind trust and you're stuck with all that uncertainty. Shock, horror: doctors don't know everything. If you want a guarantee, buy a toaster.

Or we can go back to the good old days and harness the power of faith and expectation over the human mind, with Dr Phil's Magical Healing Love Tablets. My Love Tablets are 100 per cent natural, from me. They harness all the paraphysical healing energy of every druid, fairy and deity in all the known universes, which spirals down like a vortex, through my third eye and out through my magical tablet maker.

I swear that if everyone took one of my Love Tablets every day, you'd all feel better and we'd save the NHS. All you have to do is believe.

So hands up who wants to buy my book? . . . Bastards. And who wants my Magical Healing Love Tablet? . . . Excellent. You'll do. Hand out. Swallow it. Don't chew, just swallow. Trust me.

Oh you haven't. Really? Bugger. I don't know what's in them. I just found them hanging round the clap clinic. Could be anything. But that's the point I'm trying to make. You'll do anything a doctor says.

We'd better keep an eye on you, in case you get nasty side-effects. Do we have any proper doctors in the house? You're all pissed. Fair enough. Any nurses? No? Anyone from the Philippines? OK, anyone who's seen a recent episode of *ER*, come to the front. *Holby City? Emmerdale? Animal Hospital?* How about a medical student?

Gropers, Bodgers, Gingers

Why do we trust doctors? I know most of us are decent, if psychologically flawed, doing our best in difficult circumstances. But the point is we're human. So a percentage of doctors will be gropers, bodgers, murderers and ginger. The Hippocratic oath is no vaccination against evil.

You have to trust us a bit. If we spent all day proving we're not the next Shipman, we'd never see any patients. But you could do your bit to weed out the fumblers.

I don't want to bore you with too many quotes from my bestselling book, *Trust Me, I'm a Doctor*, but here's one from a woman in Lincoln Crown Court who'd been molested by a casualty officer: 'He started kissing my stomach. I only realised he wasn't acting as a proper doctor when he did the breast examination with his mouth.'

Kissing the stomach – that's just something idiosyncratic they do in Lincoln. Breast examination with the mouth – that's one too far.

A consultant gynaecologist was struck off for making women strip naked and crawl across the floor on all fours, so he could assess their pelvic floor. What amazes me is not that there's the odd dodgy gynaecologist – no profession's perfect – but what woman in her right mind would do that?

'And bark like a dog.'

The correct response if a doctor ever asks you to play dog is 'show me first'.

There's a medical acronym, the TUBE, or 'totally unnecessary breast examination'. Something doctors might laugh about in the mess but you hope they wouldn't do it. When we filmed the highly successful BBC2 series *Trust Me, I'm a Doctor* – book of the same name available after the show – we stopped women in the street and asked them if they'd ever had their breasts examined by a doctor and not understood why. One in three. Anyone here been to the doctor with a tickly cough or a verruca, and he's said, 'While you're here, I may as well examine your breasts'? . . . Just you, sir.

The best thing you can say about a TUBE is that it won't kill you but the health service might. The NHS itself is one of the biggest causes of premature death and disease in the UK, which is a tragedy or an opportunity. If you're a florist. Each day, a jumbo jet-load of patients goes down due to preventable errors. That's a whole Shipman's-worth a day, and nobody bats an eyelid. Maybe if doctors were like pilots and we died with our patients, we'd take a bit more care. I'd have crashed and burned in 1987. And every year since.

All health services damage 10 per cent of their patients and no one's quite sure what to do about it. Why not market it? You're 177,000 times more likely to die or be harmed going into an NHS hospital than you are to win the National Lottery. That's got to be worth a punt. They should sell scratch-and-snuff cards in the League of Friends' shop.

I know a mortuary technician who works out his numbers for the lottery by seeing which of his drawers are full on Friday afternoon: '. . . six, sixteen, twenty-seven and one more for the Thunderball.'

Trusty Euphemisms

One reason you trust doctors is because you think we tell you the truth. But medicine has historically been about disguising, sanitising and spinning the truth. Gently coercing you into the treatment we think is best. All for your own good. We assume you don't want the whole truth because it isn't compatible with trust. Generally, it's not considered sensible to tell you how much we drink, how inexperienced we are or how physically attractive or repugnant we find you. And especially not what your front bottom looks like after childbirth. So we use euphemisms:

- 'You've got a little bit of a problem down below' means 'A grenade's gone off in here'.
- 'You may feel a bit of gentle prodding' means 'I take a size eighteen glove'.
- 'Yes, of course I've done one of these before' means 'I've seen it on *ER*'.
- 'You've got a spot on the lung' means 'You're going to die'.
- 'It'll get a little worse before it gets a little better' means 'You're going to die today'.
- 'It's probably a virus' means 'Go away'.
- 'It's probably a virus but we'd better examine you anyway' means 'You have fabulous breasts'.

- 'Take this drug and your risk of death will be slashed by 40 per cent' means 'If you swallow 1,825 of these over five years and at a prescription cost of £500, your risk of death would fall by 0.9 per cent. The recognised side-effects are muscle damage, headache, abdominal pain, nausea, vomiting, hairloss, anaemia, dizziness, depression, nerve damage, hepatitis, jaundice, pancreatitis and hypersensitivity syndrome'.

In return, you lie to us:
- 'I eat like a sparrow . . . Like an eighteen-stone sparrow.'
- 'I always wear a condom . . . on my head at parties.'
- 'I exercise regularly . . . if you count masturbation.'
- 'I've only just noticed the lump . . . I've been living in terror for the last six months and I'm only here now because it's started to smell.'

Medicine is a performance art, more soft spin than hard science. Don't spoil it by insisting on too much truth.

When Jimmy Savile Met the Pope

Standing up to doctors is fine until you're sick, and then you just want to have blind faith in whoever's charging at you in off-white. I am probably one of the world's greatest doctors. I think we're all agreed on that. But I have a dark secret. I'm rubbish with my hands. I knew years ago I was destined for GP land, and I'm bloody good. You stick me in a tweed jacket behind a desk – 'There's a lot of it about'; 'It's probably a virus' – and I am brilliant. Dr Empathy. I can get you in and out the door in five minutes with a smile on your face. 'Have you tried NHS Direct?' See? But please don't make me do highly technical things with my hands.

The recurring problem with the NHS is that we promise more than we can deliver. We pretend to have a fully comprehensive, high-quality service, free at the front door, without ever having the staff to do it. So we force people into doing jobs they're not best suited for. My first job as a GP trainee was working on a special care baby unit. And I did it in the south-west, where women plan to have their breech twins in a tepee on an ancient burial monument. They're pissed off coming into hospital and distraught if the baby goes on to special care. So imagine their relief when there to meet them is Dr Ten Thumbs.

The one useful thing they taught me at medical school is that when you're asked to do something that's way beyond your competence and you're shitting your pants, you put on 'the mask of relaxed brilliance'. So there I am, day one on SCBU, mask on, and this twenty-eight-week baby comes in, pretty sick, and I'm trying to get a tube down into the lungs. Hard enough for Dr Ten Thumbs without earth mother putting a lump of amethyst next to her baby. For the paraphysical healing energy. 'Oh for f-f-f-f— fine.' Nearly let the mask slip there.

Next day she brings in a lock of horsehair, then some Venezuelan healing beads. From Glastonbury. Day three and she brings in her mate the homeopath who wants to give the baby some arnica, to help bring out the bruising. Next up, a phrenologist comes in to feel the baby's skull. This bloke just sticks his dirty mitts in, dislodges a few tubes and tells Mum that the baby has very strong bones. Still the baby looks very ill.

In desperation, Mum brings in a picture of the Pope, whacks it on the side of the incubator and goes off for a coffee. I was feeling a bit light-headed by then and for some reason I got out a yellow physiotherapy card and cut out a Jimmy Savile wig for the Pope. It quite suited him. Mum comes back unexpectedly and Sister, quick as a flash, takes off the wig and turns it upside down.

'What's that?' asks Mum.

'It's Dr Phil's lucky yellow horseshoe,' says Sister. 'He made it especially.'

From that moment, the baby gets miraculously better. Off the ventilator, putting on weight and heading for the exit. They're knitting jodhpurs with lucky yellow horseshoes on, they want me to be a godfather, they want to name the baby after me. I try to explain that Gingerballs isn't a great name. For a girl. But it's all down to me and my magical healing horseshoe. They want to believe it. They don't want to know the truth. Who would? Jimmy Savile's mullet saved your baby.

Trust Me, I'm a Politician

So there are some stages in life where we need to have blind trust in doctors. But what about politicians?

Who danced naked in the rain when Labour promised all that extra money for the NHS? Who thought, 'Yes! Finally! We'll be the envy of the world'? . . . No one? OK. Who thought, 'Maybe the NHS might get a little bit better at a hundred billion pounds a year'? . . . Two of you. And who thought the money would be sucked up in mindless bureaucracy, hare-brained reforms and private plundering? . . . I'm not sure if that's cynicism or hindsight.

If the last sixty years of the NHS have taught us anything, it's that politicians shouldn't be in charge of it. They think the NHS is only made up of waiting lists and shiny new hospitals. Less of one, more of the other and you're sorted. Never mind the chronically sick, mentally ill and elderly. They don't have ribbons.

To be fair, politicians are full of brilliant ideas. Put them in charge and you get a continuous cycle of the bloody things. Untried, untested tinkering. Change, change, change. It's a neat trick. It depresses the workforce, until they're too stressed to complain, while the Health Secretary argues things really will get better 'when the next cycle of change kicks in'. And when it doesn't, you just bring in a new Health Secretary.

How can one person, sitting in a box in Whitehall, be in

charge of a million and a quarter people? As well as being a constituency MP and a postman. The whole model is stuffed from the start.

The extra money wasn't even planned. Labour wasted the first four years sticking to Tory spending plans. Then in the winter of 2001, Lord Winston's mother fell out of an NHS bed and he had a strop in the *New Statesman* about how we spend even less of our GDP on health than Poland. Blair panicked and promised to bring NHS spending up to European levels. He didn't clear it with his Cabinet, he just announced it on *Frost*. Don't you love consensus politics?

You can't suddenly pour money into the NHS and expect it to get better. After a drought, rain skids off the surface and goes down the drain. It's like shopping with Elton John. You spend a fortune on window dressing but when the money runs out, you're still Elton John. Nothing's changed. Unless you get rid of the layers of bureaucracy and the Stalinist command and control, the NHS just soaks up the extra dosh.

And you never get any decent debates about health because our political system is so childishly adversarial. Labour hated PFI and privatisation in opposition but loves them in government. All the parties hate each other too much to agree on anything. The brightest politicians on all sides could agree a consensus plan for the NHS but they won't. It would take the futility out of politics.

Besides, Blair couldn't even convince his Cabinet about NHS reform, never mind the Labour Party. Brown hated Blair, Blair hated Brown. Blair announced his NHS plan, Brown trumped it with one from Derek Wanless, a retired bank manager. Can Captain Mainwairing save the NHS? No, because he's been trumped again by Professor Darzi, a specialist in robot-assisted surgery. Who'll be saving the NHS next week? Bagpuss?

Rationing

About the only thing politicians agree on is never to use the word 'rationing'. We've always had the most rationed health service of any Western democracy. Fewer hospitals, fewer beds, fewer doctors and nurses, fewer drugs, fewer machines that go 'ping'. Frank Dobson once let the R-word slip, when restricting Viagra to those men at risk of falling out of bed. But then he was sacked.

The reason politicians don't admit to rationing is they'd then have to admit to all the people who've died prematurely in the history of the NHS, because they've been denied access to a good standard of care. Politicians have killed millions more people than doctors ever could, and that's going some. The Cenotaph isn't just a memorial to the war dead; it's in between the Department of Health and the Treasury. That's not a coincidence.

And, of course, health care is a bottomless pit. The NHS was founded on 5 July 1948. Prior to that, rich people had health insurance and saw the top specialists, while the chronically sick, mentally ill and highly infectious were left to die in government-funded workhouse hospitals. There's progress for you.

The theory was that as we got fitter on the NHS, we'd use it less. But the elderly were quietly sitting at home deaf, blind, edentulous and without health care. First they got hearing aids and tuned in to the nagging.

'You ought to go and get your eyes checked.'

Then they got the glasses.

'God, my teeth are awful.'

Within a year, the NHS was on its knees with the bill for *sans*-everything war pensioners. It's never recovered. There's always new technology and old patients to take all the money away.

Rationing isn't always a bad thing. An eighteen-month wait

for surgery in some hospitals can increase your life expectancy by, oh, eighteen months.

Safe with Us

Politicians have always excelled at spin. Nye Bevan gave us 'Cradle to grave'. Sounds great until you realise you've been yanked out of the cradle and stuck in the grave a tad prematurely. Thatcher said 'the National Health Service is safe with us' and then dropped it on the floor and kicked it round the living room for eleven years. Virginia Bottomley founded a 'good news unit' to spread the word of people who'd actually survived the NHS. Then Stephen Fry spotted an anagram of her name is 'I'm an evil Tory bigot' and she was never heard of again. Alan Milburn assured us 'the NHS is not for sale' before flogging off hospitals and clinical services to private companies. John Reid celebrated his new job with 'Oh fuck, not health', did a passable impression of Gollum and opposed the smoking ban on the grounds that poor people had the right to die prematurely. Which left the way open for the delightful Patsy Hewitt, whose towering twin epitaphs – 'the NHS has never had it so good' and 'a penny wasted is a penny stolen from a patient' – are still guaranteed to bring the house down at a Royal College of Nursing conference.

And now, the English NHS has Alan 'Postie' Johnson, who glibly announced that the increase in life expectancy since the war (presumably Germany, not Iraq) is entirely due to the NHS and 'great scientific advances'. Life expectancies also tend to increase after wars because fewer people are blown up. And a tour of his beloved, flooded Hull should at least have dropped the odd penny. Which makes you live longer, a visit to the GP or removing shit from your living room?

Privates on Parade

Gordon Brown loves the Private Finance Initiative, because it keeps the spending on new hospitals off the balance sheet. But what a rip-off. Why pay 30 per cent interest on a new hospital when you can get 4 per cent at Nationwide? PFI hospitals are £100 million a year in debt before they've opened their doors. So they need to get all the business they can. Only they've got fewer beds, so they're full to bursting with patients. And MRSA. The design and build quality is questionable, they get boiling in the summer, it's absurdly bureaucratic to change any cock-ups and NHS staff have no control over hospitals they don't own. When it all goes tits up, they'll be flogged off for housing and we'll have no hospitals at all. Apart from that, it's a great use of public money. PFI – pay for it indefinitely.

And why are we paying private overseas companies staffed by foreign surgeons to cherry-pick easy operations when the NHS desperately needs the work? Why give them guaranteed contracts paid above the going rate, whether they do the work or not? Why not just give NHS hospitals the money to treat patients locally and follow them up? Why let a dodgy hand surgeon fly in from Germany, whack in a dodgy hip with no cement and be safely back in Hamburg by the time it falls out?

And why are we importing doctors and exporting patients? Why are we sending old women over to France to get their hips done? Some have never been abroad before but off they go, on the bruise cruise, clutching their phrasebooks. 'Does it have to be a suppository, doctor?'

Why? Because Labour believes NHS surgeons are an evil cartel of self-protective money-grabbers intent on keeping waiting lists as long as possible so they can cream off the private work. True, there's the odd orthopod camping down at BUPA and the odd gynaecologist with a golden speculum. But most surgeons are simple folk. They just want to operate and get people better. The trick is to stop them when they're past their sell-by date. Otherwise, it's carnage.

Waiting list reductions are a good thing. When I trained, the waiting list drawer was a mile long and you were more likely to die on it than reach the front. Patients would bite your hand off to help in exams because they'd be bumped up the list. Twenty rough rectal examinations followed by tea and biscuits was a small price to pay.

But waiting times have come down largely thanks to work done in NHS hospitals. Yet we'll have wasted a fortune on unnecessary private competition of dubious quality. Money that could have gone to dementia and herpes.

Filling the Holes

Labour also believes people need more access to health. So they've taken nurses off the wards and stuck them behind a phone line. NHS Direct. Patients love it, of course they do. Thousands of calls a day. We're becoming a nation with an unhealthy obsession with health. But instead of basing it in GPs' surgeries and getting everyone to cooperate, it was set up on its own to threaten the evil cartel of GPs who never tell their patients anything. But it won't reduce the NHS workload. The more calls you take, the more anxiety you generate, the more you don't want to be sued, the more you refer to a doctor.

I shouldn't be too harsh. It's great if you've been out for a few beers, you come home and there's nothing on the telly. Phone up NHS Direct, tell them you've swallowed a wing nut and listen to the nurse chase down that algorithm: 'Wing nut, wing nut, wing nut, wing nut, wing nut, wing nut, wing nut . . . um, would you say it's diabetes at all?' Endless hours of family fun.

And the access doesn't stop there. GPs are practising out of corrugated shacks with leaking roofs. So let's spend millions on spanking new walk-in centres. Walk in anytime and be told you need to see your GP. And now you can, within twenty-four hours, whether you need to or not.

'What can I do for you?'

'I've got the sniffles.'

'How long have you had them?'

'Since breakfast.'

And if you don't want to wait twenty-four hours, you can now be treated in casualty within four. 'Oooh. A paper cut. That does look nasty.'

All these new points of access have turned the NHS into a beast with seven arseholes. There are just so many new ways to end up in the shit. Now we just have to find a way of measuring the level.

Stars in Your PFIs

Quality control in the NHS is a good thing. It wasn't Labour's idea – it was forced on them by parents who campaigned for a public inquiry into the Bristol heart disaster. With fifty years of NHS chaos and underfunding, no one checked we were cutting babies' hearts open properly. A small oversight.

We need to find out what the best treatments are, check we're doing them properly and publish the results. But we need to all grow up so we don't stop surgeons taking on the sickest patients or divert even more NHS money to lawyers. Above all, it mustn't be overly simplistic. So what did Labour come up with? Star charts.

When the *Egon Ronay Guide to Hospitals* first came out, I was living in a little Bermuda Triangle in the south-west of England. My three nearest hospitals were the Royal United in Bath, Weston General and the Bristol Royal Infirmary. Not one bloody star between the three of them. And I'd worked in all three. Could have been cause and effect but it's a small sample.

I went into the casualty department at the BRI and asked Sister what it was like for staff morale working in a zero-star trust. She said, 'Off the record, we quite like it. No stars means no expectations. People come in here expecting to die. And often they do.'

So maybe the way to save the NHS is to lower public expectations, so we can match them. Instead of 'The NHS: Safe in our Hands' we should rebrand it 'The NHS: Shit Happens'. Put 'Shit Happens' above every hospital, surgery and walk-in centre in the land. Give the staff little badges with 'Shit Happens' on them. It's got to be worth a pilot, surely? We could start in Bristol.

Bristol is now an excellent place to have heart surgery. The one place another Bristol won't happen again is Bristol. But Labour is keen it won't happen anywhere else either, so they proposed a rigorous new quality control system. Can you guess? Yes, star charts for heart surgeons. You know when you go into McDonald's and the bloke serving you has no stars on his badge? You assume he's pissing in the milkshakes. Who in their right mind is going to choose a zero-star heart surgeon?

Half of all doctors will always be below average. What matters is that there's an agreed standard you audit your work against and if you fall below that, someone quickly checks if it's down to sick patients, statistical error, bad luck, poor teamwork, dodgy equipment, alcohol, depression, alcohol and depression or a workaholic surgeon with a narcissistic personality disorder who refuses to be wrong.

Labour has now ditched star charts but still hasn't stopped non-specialist surgeons dabbling in occasional, highly complex operations and getting far worse results than specialist centres. Quality and safety have been buried under competition, privatisation and political cowardice.

You've Been Quangoed

Quality control needs to be independent of the NHS brotherhood. Someone to tell us the right thing to do, based on the best evidence, and someone to check we're doing it right. Keep it simple and local, and spend the money on patients. Instead, Labour's gone quango mad. We've had an Audit

Commission, a Healthcare Commission, a Commission for Public and Patient Involvement in Health, a National Clinical Assessment Service, a National Institute of Health and Clinical Excellence, a National Patient Safety Agency, an NHS Modernisation Agency, an NHS University and an NHS Leadership Centre. Sorry if I've missed a few. Dozen. Some have crashed and burned. Others just shout at us from very expensive boxes somewhere.

They fly around the world, learning from the Inuit and buy in management consultants to come up with a miracle top-down fix for the NHS. Here's one: set your sights a bit lower. Instead of NICE – National Institute of Health and Clinical Excellence – why not NIGE: the National Institute of Good Enough? 'Oh sod it, that'll do.' I'm happy for NICE to tell me what to do on one condition: it evaluates all the reforms, quangos and consultancies with the same scientific rigour and weeds out all the ones that can't prove their cost-effective benefit to patients.

The Department of Chaos

Let's start with the Department of Health. According to the Cabinet Office, it's the second most dysfunctional government department (after the ho-ho-Home Office). I went to the DoH once, by mistake. Alan Milburn invited 'media medics' into his lair to try and get us all onside with the NHS plan. When he realised I was *Private Eye*'s medical correspondent, we both clammed up. It was an awkward moment. I had planned to ask him lots of difficult questions but there's a world of difference between slagging off the NHS from the comfort of your own computer and taking on an ambitious bully who's micromanaging it into oblivion.

When I got to Richmond House, the nerves kicked in and I needed to use the toilet. So I squatted down in the gents' and spotted some graffiti at eye level: 'There are 2,000 people working in the Department of Health, and at this precise moment you're the only one who knows what he's doing.'

What's the point of the Department of Health? People working in silos typing away feverishly about 'choice' or 'access' or 'clinical accountability' or 'deliberative, distributive democracy'. But none of the dots join up. The DoH is like some great sponge that sucks up all the money and ideas, with the odd dribble getting through to the front line.

The NHS is Worth Saving, not Americanising

If I had to single out one politician responsible for the state of the NHS, it'd be Winston Churchill. If he hadn't won the war, we'd have a health service like the Germans'. Not that we want one. The service to patients in the NHS isn't that bad. Ask people what they think of the NHS as reported in the press, they'll say it's crap. Ask people what their experiences of the NHS are, and most say it's great. Or at least adequate. Slagging off the NHS is like Joni Mitchell hitting a watermelon with a sledge hammer. We won't know what we've got till it's gone.

The beauty of it is that it's a one-stop shop, free at the front door. If you're run over or stabbed, you don't have to check your wallet before you get in the ambulance. When you have your brain tumour removed, you aren't kicked out the next day because your insurance policy doesn't cover continuing care. Whatever happens to the NHS, we don't want to Americanise it. No large companies cherry-picking easy operations and leaving those too sick to turn a profit to die in casualty. Or preferably just outside.

In all countries with insurance systems, the sickest patients are those without insurance. Let's not go there.

The signs aren't good. Having hated the Tories' evil internal market in opposition, Labour wants to recreate it. Hospitals now have sweatshops full of coders, logging every single item of care, so a bill can be sent to the Primary Care Trust who will return it with queries because it hasn't got any money. The NHS has been technically bankrupt since the bill arrived for glasses, dentures and hearing aids in 1949. This obsession with invoicing is just a very expensive way of proving it.

The first question you get asked as you enter a beautiful, gleaming, no-expense-spared American hospital is not 'What can I do for you?' but 'How will you pay?' In America, the forty-six million without insurance either die prematurely or pitch up at the emergency room with death rattle. NHS casualty departments are also sinks for the poor who don't play the system well. Labour claims the NHS will always be free at the front door but a front door's only any use if it's (a) near your house and (b) open.

Labour plans to move the front door to hospitals further away. We can't have poor people with no transport clogging up our casualty departments. So let's close them down. At least the ones not in marginal Labour constituencies. Hospitals already shut the door on those patients the PCT won't fund.

Some specialist services like brain surgery need to be concentrated on fewer sites but the treatment of common emergencies such as asthma, choking, drowning and anaphylaxis is best done closer to home. There's hardly a glut of ambulances out there. And who wants a two-hour dash to hospital, stuck behind a tractor?

In such a politicised system, you can't separate the ideology from the evidence. Labour Cabinet members and frontbench MPs have joined arms around their constituency hospitals and opposed their own health policy. And we're expected to accept it. Labour hopes putting a senior robotically assisted surgeon in charge of hospital reconfiguration will be enough to convince us. It won't. You need to publish all the evidence for and against hospital closures and let an independent body like NICE analyse it.

Market competition may close down hospitals and split up

the NHS monopoly but with it goes the one-stop shop. Whoever bids lowest gets the contract. You'll end up going all over town for different bits of care, treated by strangers you keep telling the same story to in the hope they can understand you. Health care is built on the human relationships you develop, over time, with the staff you meet. Continuity is vital. Getting your cholesterol done at Tesco isn't.

The Biggest IT Cock-up in the World, Ever

Labour pretends we're going to have a fabulous new computer system ('the largest in the world, ever!') that allows any doctor or nurse to access your records anywhere from Tesco to Timbuktu. But we know it'll be a multibillion-pound disaster because . . .

- it's the NHS
- it's computers
- it's centrally managed by workaholic control freaks in a box in London, rather than engaging and trusting the ingenuity of NHS staff to find a system that works for them.

Choose and Book

Choose and book is a convoluted procedure aimed at allowing you to be seen at a hospital of your choice at a time of your choosing. Only you're not given any meaningful information as to how to compare one hospital with another. However, you do get a unique twelve-digit booking reference number and ridiculous password ('cake counter', 'broccoli spot', 'fountain saver' . . .). Sometimes it works, sometimes it doesn't. Could the money be better spent elsewhere? They somehow manage the NHS in Wales, Scotland and Northern Ireland without it (and without foundation trusts, connecting for health, payment by results, practice-based commissioning, tariff unbundling or whatever other new reform is invented to soak up the extra funding).

Who stands to gain most from all this NHS investment? The private sector. They can sniff it a mile off. Buildings, building maintenance, catering, supplies, IT systems, clinical services, consultancies, inducements, sweeteners, jobs for the boys. The stench of Brown's extra billions has carried all the way to America. But is Labour clever enough to stand up to a private sector they hated in opposition and know very little about? Who says yes? . . . Just you, sir. And who do you work for? . . . McKinsey. Splendid.

Who's Got the Power?

Good anything (health care, politics, sex) depends on the responsible use of power. Good health reforms would engage the staff, allowing them to participate and consent. Bad reforms are like being shafted roughly from behind over a damp beanbag. Whether you want it or not.

If we want to save the NHS, we need to find who's in power and make sure they're using it responsibly. Simple. But no one will admit to having power. Ask the doctors, they'll say it's the politicians. Go to the Department of Health and they'll say it's the Treasury. Go the Treasury and they'll say it's Downing Street. Go to Downing Street and some Campbell clone will punch you in the throat.

While you're waiting for an ambulance, he'll say power is shared by an evil triumvirate of doctors, lawyers and journalists but we're going to give it to patients. Ask a patient and he'll say, 'I don't want power, I just want my throat fixed by a good surgeon, in a clean local hospital, with a nice smiley nurse who speaks English. Oh, and somewhere to park. For free. And will the ambulance be here soon?'

Power in the NHS is always over the next hill, so to save it we need to cut down on the hills. Let's start by kicking out the politicians, storming the Department of Health and selling off the quangos for sheltered housing. Are you with me?

OK. So who's going to run it? How about the medical establishment?

Not so keen on that, are we? Bring back the politicians.

GMC, RIP

I'm embarrassed to have to be regulated by the General Medical Council. And pay good money for it. They seem to have missed the boat on every major medical scandal that's happened in the last twenty years. Ironically, they've now formed a rapid response force which is meeting this evening to decide whether to take action. Against Dr Crippen. There's a bit of a backlog.

They've also rebranded themselves in true Labour style. They're now known as 'the new GMC – all Shipman shape and Bristol fashion'.

Let's pretend Shipman wasn't a mass murderer, just a very, very incompetent GP. Would he have been picked up any quicker? No. You'd have thought when he wiped out a whole terrace, somebody might have said, 'Maybe he's not terribly good. Maybe we need to look into this.'

Shipman knew he could get away with it. When he was done for drugs in 1987, he told *GP* magazine, 'The system is so slow, a doctor could die of old age before he goes up in front of the GMC.' People in the GMC die of old age too. It's an elephants' graveyard.

The GMC hasn't got a clue what's going on in the front line. You can't regulate doctors from a box in London. Or it could be Manchester. They may have moved. I haven't really got a clue where the GMC is. Shouldn't be long now.

The Royal Colleges

If you don't know what the Royal Colleges do, you're in good company. They don't either. In theory, they're supposed to be there for every specialty to define and monitor standards of training. In reality, they're somewhere you go when you're too senile for the BMA but not quite senile enough for the GMC.

But they are very good at collecting wine. If you're a junior doctor, trying to pass your exams, they fail you the first few times and use your exam fees for claret. But when you finally make it into the club, you're a member for life. You could butcher a busload of grannies and still be on the Christmas card list. All the dodgy doctors that the GMC finally gets round to striking off retain their membership of their college. 'And over here is the Hackers' Lounge . . .'

I was asked to give a talk at the Royal College of Surgeons, by mistake. I thought, 'I'm only going to get one go at the buggers,' so I called my talk 'Are You Any Good at It, Doctor?' They loved me. As luck would have it, the front page of the *Express* that morning was 'Butcher Surgeon Killed my Wife'. So I held it up in front of the old farts and asked them what they thought.

'Bloody disgusting, bloody media, bloody tabloids, bloody scum, bloody, bloody, bloody, bloody, bloody, bloody, bloody.'

'This is about Rodney Ledward, the self-styled fastest gynaecologist in the south-east. The nurses called him butcher, not the journalists. Have you ever worked with a really dodgy doctor and a nickname to match?'

'Butcher Bates!'

'Chopper Charlton!'

'Hacker Harris . . . Hackety, hackety, hackety, hack . . . Duck!'

'Fine. How many of you reported your concerns to the GMC? How many of you acted promptly to protect patients from unnecessary harm?'

'Oh, no no no no no no no! Thou shalt not disparage another doctor.'

The one perk of being a doctor is the inside knowledge. We know who we'd send Mum to and who we wouldn't send the dog to. But we're not telling you. Because he's a very nice man who's given his life to the NHS and we don't want to screw up his pension.

How many people here work in the NHS? Hands up? Keep your hand up if you know someone you wouldn't let within five feet of you with anything sharp. Almost all of us. Keep your hand up if you've done something about it.

There's a doctor up north known locally as the Terminator. Could just be a harmless term of endearment. A friend of mine worked in a hospital with a bloke called Killer Keane. There were concerns about his competence but instead of investigating them, they wrote a song about him in the Christmas show. That's self-regulation for you. We do it by gossip, innuendo and Christmas revue. They rewrote 'Killer Queen':

> He keeps bits of his patients
> In jars out in the potting shed
> No one complains about him
> Well how could they, they're all dead?
> Chop chop chopper-tee-chop
> Hacketee hacketee hack
> If he gets you on the table
> Then you ain't coming back
> He's a Killer Keane
> Don't look know there goes me spleen
> He'd did for me dad and me Aunty Jean
> Guaranteed to flatline
> Ev'ry time!

How we all laughed. If you've got an operation coming up, and you want to find out if your surgeon's any good, don't ask the

Royal Colleges or the GMC because they won't tell you even if they knew. Just pop along to the next hospital revue. If he's that bad, they'll be singing about it.

Talk to senior surgeons and they'll wax lyrical about the post-war years, when we made huge advances in organ transplants and heart surgery. But there was a very steep learning curve. People who hadn't given their lives for their country gave their lives to the NHS as guinea pigs in the name of medical progress. If the Germans don't get you, the surgeons will. What does it matter? We're all going to die anyway.

And this 'see one, do one, teach one' culture filtered down into training. Junior surgeons were left alone to do major ops for the first time with their consultants not even in the hospital. The Royal Colleges didn't bat an eyelid. It's the only way to learn, apparently.

The trouble with all hierarchies is that to get to the top, you have to be a yes-man, you have to lick arse all the way up. So if you finally reach the summit, you're completely incapable of changing anything for the people lower down. Which is why the Royal Colleges represent junior doctors so badly.

And the BMA. Junior doctor firebrands morph into tedious grey-suited conformists and then professional nest-featherers on their way to a knighthood. They talk tough when it comes to protecting their wallets but sell junior doctors down the river.

'What do we want?'

'We're not sure.'

'When do we want it?'

'Whenever you tell us.'

The government has tried to reform the medical establishment, with predictably disastrous results. One man in a box telling another man in a box what to do. We've been dithering over MOTs for doctors for the best part of a decade but no one can decide what makes a good doctor and how that should be measured. The centralised, computerised reforms of job applications created 10,000 suicidal junior doctors and no guarantee that the best candidates got the right jobs. Here's a thought: let senior doctors have local control over who they appoint; they have to sort out the consequences if they take on a duffer. And have someone local and independent of the NHS analysing errors and complaints quickly and fairly. Give the medical establishment and the Department of Health as little to do as possible. It's much safer that way.

Better still, close it down and convert all those lovely prime London locations into nurses' homes. Or maybe nursing homes. No, they already are.

Managers

OK, so we've kicked out the politicians, the civil servants and the medical establishment. Which leaves managers to save the NHS. You're not too keen on that either. What do you get if you cross an NHS manager with a pig? Nothing: there are some things even a pig won't do.

NHS managers aren't allowed to manage. They're just toys for ministers. They used to have to stick to budget and persecute whistleblowers. Now they have to hit targets as well. Labour pretends to hand power to the front line but controls everything. They centralise praise and devolve blame. If you don't hit my targets, you're fired, not me.

One of my local hospitals had two stars until it was discovered that in order to meet their casualty waiting time target, they'd been hiding critically ill patients in the back of ambulances. There's so much time pressure on casualty staff that they're now treating targets rather than patients. If you end up with the wrong diagnosis on the wrong ward in three hours and fifty-nine minutes, you're a success. Right diagnosis, right ward, four hours and one second: failure. 'What a time to have a cardiac arrest. You could cost me my job, you sick bastard.'

Targets are fine if you limit them, agree them with the staff and make sure they don't contradict each other or stuff patients with less politically sexy illnesses. But the time frames in the NHS are ridiculously rushed. Everything has to be done by the next big political speech or conference. It's impossible but your job depends on it. Either you kill yourself, you throw money at it and send the hospital spiralling into debt, or you pretend to hit the targets. Shred the waiting lists and hide patients in the cupboard under the stairs. I know what I'd do.

Targets need a bit of intelligent leeway. The NHS is supposed to treat according to clinical need but the less sick regularly leapfrog over the more sick because they're in danger of breaching a waiting-time target. And the poor waiting-list manager gets it in the neck from everyone.

Too many targets take away the ability of clinical staff to think for themselves and create a tribe of clipboarded bureaucrats ticking off the boxes. Add in the computerised coding and billing of every single item of care and you have hell on earth. If you don't believe me, look in the job section at the back of the *Health Service Journal*. Just what does the Quality Monitoring Officer for the Contracts' Facilitator in the Care Services' Directorate do? If he told you, you wouldn't understand.

Thatcher started it. She got in Roy 'Grocer' Griffiths from Sainsbury's. We're going through the whole cast of *Dad's Army* now. He told her the NHS needed more managers. That's because he had a few thousand he needed to offload. We've now got more of the buggers than beds.

But what are they for? How many people here, working in the NHS, have recently been praised or motivated by their managers? Who would say they have a leader, a visionary guiding and inspiring them through the most expensive and largest reform programme in NHS history? . . . No one? Who's even met their chief executive? . . . Just you, madam. And what do you do? . . . You're a chief executive. Jesus.

The NHS needs management, not managers. If we get rid of the politicians and the civil servants, we can halve the targets and the managers. Then with all the money we save we'll buy a few really good ones. And we'd still have enough left to double the pay of the nurses. Are you with me?

How about Tesco?

Would the NHS be better if it was run by Tesco? It won't be long now. Labour reckons the NHS could do with the 'constructive discomfort' of private competition and if we start that game, there'll only be one winner.

Mind you, I can just see myself in a little peaked cap, in between the chunky chickens and the Mediterranean vegetables. 'Hello, I'm Tesco's Dr Phil, how may I heal you? We've got two smears for the price of one, until 7 November only, and there's an all-you-can-swallow vitamin bar next to the cut-price muffins.'

Private companies move fast and respond quickly because they have to. Otherwise they go bust. The NHS moves at the speed of a glacier because attached to the rock of front-line staff is a huge, bloated, self-protective, indestructible, money-burning, Stalinist limpet that would have been bankrupt years ago if only anyone had done the accounts properly.

We pretend the NHS is in peril but it's far more likely to kill you. Ever tried making a complaint? Doctors can't even find your notes or X-rays, so what chance the managers? After they've shredded them? People have devoted their lives to trying to get justice and accountability out of the Limpet. After twenty years, you're lucky if you get 'sorry'. Doctors and nurses are suspended for years while the Limpet bats them to and from the courts.

Too much bureaucracy, too many people in the comfort zone. The solution is not to sell off the NHS, just hack off the Limpet. Strip out all the untested reforms, bad practice and useless bureaucracy, and hand power to the managers, clinicians and patients who are still alive, ideologically speaking. But that will take time. And effort. And we'd have to rebuild a lot of trust. And we need results for the party conference. So let's just hand it over to Tesco or McKinsey or KPMG or United Health or Kaiser or whoever's saturated the market in their own country and wants to invade Europe.

Markets won't save the NHS. We need devolution, cooperation, continuity and trust. Are you with me?

Don't Go Outside

Why are we so adversarial and negative? Probably because our politicians, lawyers and journalists are. But is what they say in any way representative? Is it the truth?

As Arthur Scargill, the second finest ginger mind to grace the political stage, put it: 'What the media present as news is pure, unadulterated bias. There is no balance.'

To test out his theory, I once collected headlines for the national and local press in the Midlands for a week. After five days, I was so depressed I had to stop. So now I'm going to depress *you*. Negative points first:

Negative
- Crisis in casualty
- Deaths put spotlight on pressures facing NHS
- Patients suffering
- Crisis of care
- Cutback fears
- Don't drive a stake through the NHS
- Britain living on diet of half-truths
- Boy, 15, dies of meningitis
- Nurse told home-visit racism is legal
- Warning on advance of cell biology
- Bug fear hits sales of beef

- Black nurse loses claim on race bias
- NHS accused over mentally ill killers
- Pensioner loses home fight
- More will go private in NHS bed crisis
- Hospital bed crisis will get worse
- Extra 1,500 died in cold at Christmas
- Chained night and day: the prisoner with HIV
- NHS swamped with elderly who can't afford to keep warm
- Hospital runs out of meningitis vaccine
- Nurse shortage deprives children of intensive care
- Community care: ministers blamed
- Health warning: do not get ill
- Vaccine runs out after mass meningitis jabs
- Stay away plea on 'brain bug' hospital
- Smoking is 'inherited' by young
- Women miss out on cancer test
- Health alert over bacteria that resist drugs
- Psychiatrists quit over risks to patients
- Psychiatric beds under siege from all sides
- Community-care patient found dead after killing mum
- OAPs face care grants ban
- Document fuels fears over bed shortage
- Brain illness kills city baby
- Doctors demand new security from attack
- Gridlock in secure beds adds to crisis on the wards
- Op cancelled by lecture tour surgeon
- Fertility clinic set to destroy 3,000 orphan embryos
- Meningitis strikes 12-week-old baby
- 'Killer bug' fear on wards
- Dentists: are they putting profitability before patients?
- Hospital struggles to meet dialysis need
- Medical research facing new cuts
- Home is closed by council

- Acne drug blamed for two deaths
- Private health hits NHS
- Psychiatric ward close to despair
- Complaints about NHS trusts top 100,000
- Kidney patient given cancerous transplant
- NHS managers up 400 per cent

It's all right. You can breathe again now. Here are the positive headlines:

Positive
- Embarrassed regional health chief keeps his job
- Murders by mentally ill 'show no increase'
- Struck-off matron can go back to nursing job
- Snake venom offers hope of thrombosis cure

Thanks to the NHS
Evolutionary biologists believe our obsession with bad news helps us avoid danger but I think it just makes us depressed. Does my list reflect your experience of the NHS in an average week? Here are my unpublished headlines from the same week:

- Doctor removes wart (successfully)
- Woman with flu gets better without antibiotics
- Doctor receives jar of chutney from grateful patient (see wart story)
- Doctor gives jar of chutney to receptionist for good service

Wonderful stories like these of triumph over adversity and the generosity of human spirit occur in surgeries up and down the country every day. And do we ever hear about them? There was only one really positive headline in my study from the letters page of the *Leicester Mercury,* from a Mrs D. Chalk from Oadby:

Thanks to the NHS

I agree with B. G. Robinson. Local hospitals treated my late husband better than any private one could ever have done. Even though he met a premature end due to a medication overdose, I had no complaints. Anyone can make a mistake.

With the insurance paying off the mortgage and the compensation I received, I have been able to purchase a modest apartment in Majorca. So even the darkest clouds can have a silver lining, thanks to the NHS.

Mrs D. Chalk, Oadby

Can the Media Save the NHS?

Can we save the NHS through balanced reporting? Instead of focusing on killer bugs and wonder drugs, we could have some dull realism and modest success. First, we need to shoot the headline writers. This is from the *Morley Advertiser*, about an old lady who'd gone into hospital for surgery and was kicked out the next day because they needed the bed. And the headline? 'Daughter Disgusted by Disabled Mother's Early Morning Discharge'.

Journalists seem to struggle with science. Most of it's about the gradual accumulation of knowledge over time, not freak-show sensationalism. Remember when they cloned a human ear on the back of a mouse? I was phoned by the medical correspondent of the *Daily Express* to ask if that was to help the mouse hear better.

Even when it's done properly, media intervention seems to backfire. A team of doctors got together with the scriptwriters of BBC's *Casualty* to warn people how unpleasant it is to die from paracetamol overdose. All very graphic. After the show went out, they measured the incidence of paracetamol overdose in real casualty departments around the UK. It went up. All the happy viewers hid their paracetamol. The unhappy ones thought, 'That's the way to do it.'

MMRse

MMR. As safe a vaccine as you can get, both of my kids have had it, along with hundreds of millions of others, without coming to harm. But we'd rather believe an insignificant research finding fanned into a media über-scare. Vaccination levels drop, nasty diseases come back and the government panics.

We've seen it all with BSE. As measles spreads, there'll be a mass cull in all infected nurseries and any contiguous nurseries within a ten-mile radius. Huge bonfires of measles-infected children. But at least they didn't have the vaccine. And all because *The Lancet* is read by the health editor of the *Daily Mail*.

The media is very powerful and almost totally unaccountable, a never-ending drivel of opinion supported by error spun in the scariest or most sensational way. No one has a clue what the editors of papers or news programmes look like. If they screw up, they don't even need to hide. The worst they'll get is a small fine and a light slap from whatever regulatory panel they sit on. And you thought the GMC was bad.

Experts Have Been Known to Die

Medical researchers have become just like the rest of us, desperate for media exposure. If you feed anything to a rat in large enough quantities, either you give it cancer or you cure it of the cancer you gave it in the first place. Either way, you've got a paper in *The Lancet* and all the fame and funding it brings.

But experts have been known to get it wrong. Remember the 'BSE in sheep' scandal? Or rather non-scandal, because the experts mistook the sheep samples for the cow samples. They should get out of the lab more. The sheep are the ones without the udders.

And what about SARS? Three thousand column inches of panic, and not one death in the UK. True, it took some nifty global infection control and we had to lock up an entire hospital in Canada but it never reached us. Still, if you wanted a train to yourself, all you had to do was stick a Chinese flag on your luggage and cough.

In contrast, a hundred people a year die falling down the stairs. Every year. Why don't we have a STAIRS scare? Even more people die when they're wearing those ridiculous SARS masks because they can't see where they're going. Falls in the elderly are a better predictor of death than all the health scares put together. The least they deserve is a ribbon.

Bird flu happens to birds. It may transfer to humans but you can cut your risks by not having sex with a wild goose. Or if you do, please use a condom. If chlamydia and bird flu mix, we're all going down.

Healthy is what you are when you're not worrying about your health. Most health scares never happen. And yet they cost the NHS a fortune in panic management. Either ignore them, treat them solely as light entertainment or, if you're like me, do the opposite out of bloody-mindedness. I eat beef, use a mobile phone, vaccinate my kids and have unprotected sex with all my geese. Works for me.

Tinky Winston to the Rescue

> Tinky Winston,
> Hilary,
> Raj Raj,
> Phil.
> Teledoctors,
> Teledoctors,
> Say how much?

Can TV doctors save the NHS? I suspect not. There's a fine line between Teledoctors and *Teletubbies*. I once interviewed a professor of urogynaecology for the BBC about his research into cranberry juice and urine infections. Lights, camera, action. 'My research has unequivocally shown that *Ocean Spray* cranberry juice . . .' He just couldn't help himself. They'd sponsored his trial; he wanted to say thank you.

People assume that if you're a TV doctor, you must be better than ordinary doctors. That's why you're on the telly. But usually the reverse is true. You go in search of telly to escape the NHS, so you're deskilled and out of touch. Or is that just me?

Most people have chocolates or flowers backstage; I get this: 'Dear Dr Phil, these are my giant scabs, had for years.' I wouldn't mind but I nearly snorted them. Any ideas?

All doctors have a blind spot and mine's dermatology. When I was training to be a GP, I was embarrassed by my ignorance so I'd hide behind the curtains and look things up in a book. But these days we're supposed to be open. A bloke came in with a rash I'd never seen, so I got two textbooks down from the shelf, gave one to him and said, 'Let me know if you spot anything that looks like it.' He complained. Thought I was being flippant.

Sick Doctors
Which brings us nicely to the million or so, largely decent, hard-working, competent except in dermatology, NHS staff. Can they save the NHS?

Hello, I'm Dr Phil and I'm an alcoholic. It's all that human misery and suffering. And that's just the receptionists. But at least I don't smoke. Well, not much. I'm usually too pissed to light up.

The GMC has estimated there may be as many as 13,000 drug- and alcohol-addicted doctors in the NHS. Unfortunately, they don't know where we work. But if each of us makes 2,000 life-and-death decisions a year, that's twenty-six million vital calls made each year in the NHS by addicted doctors. Cheers!

Why do so many doctors end up sicker than their patients? Part of the problem is that doctors are psychologically peculiar to start with. If you recruit academics with three grade-A science A-levels and the people skills of a small rock, they're always going to struggle in a pool of the great unwashed. Here's a letter sent in to *Hospital Doctor* by a consultant radiologist:

> There are a substantial number of patients out there who are utterly execrable. They are, in the main, at worst trivially unwell. They need no attention, apart from a good slapping, but insist on being seen. I can only imagine the horror of seeing a waiting room filled with these churls and ingrates all bleating louder than sheep, knowing that there is damn-all wrong with them. I have a mental image of revenge, turning to a most loathsome specimen smiling thinly while declaring, 'You've got cancer, you bastard, die soon.'

Do you think he's lost his zest for clinical practice? Maybe he's on the fringes of burn-out. Some doctors just can't do the bad news bit. I once met an obstetrician whose stock line to women after a miscarriage was: 'Far better that this should happen than you have a child who's socially awkward.'

I thought that was the whole point of children.

The NHS is a very unhealthy place to work – we damage 10 per cent of the staff each year – but it's still full of workaholics. My consultants would say, 'I used to work for months on end, never saw daylight, enjoyed every second of it. Trial by fire.' And I'd look at these burned-out blobs of jaundiced protoplasm and think, 'Maybe not.'

It was a badge of honour for your car to never be out of the car park. Could just mean you were shagging your secretary, or maybe you were too pissed to drive home. Workaholism was praised but nothing else. It was largely training by humiliation. I've known doctors who are suspended or up in court, whose colleagues never ask how they're coping. One consultant was admitted for surgery and wheeled through the hospital in front of all her colleagues. Not one acknowledged her. How can a profession that claims to care have such little regard for its own?

We blame managers and politicians for not motivating the staff but you can work in the NHS all your life without receiving praise from another doctor. Doctors are their own worst enemies; we've created this sick macho culture and it's going to be tough for other doctors to lead us out of it.

Silence of the Consultants

Consultants are certainly bright enough to save the NHS but they're too peculiar and ideologically diverse to ever unite. Most believe in the ideals of the NHS but there are always some who go in search of merit awards or knighthoods and become apparatchiks for the Limpet.

Many are now too insecure about their future to take charge. Blair beat them. Like a good lawyer, he won the arguments without making things better. Bristol and Shipman were the tools to take power and control away from doctors. Consultants no longer manage their waiting lists. Panicking managers tell them they have to stop treating patients from South Yorkshire because the PCT's contract is up, or that cold cases must hop over emergencies so we can move up the star chart.

Private companies come in and strip away the easy, profitable cases. Consultants would love to work in these gleaming new MRSA-free treatment centres but they're not allowed to. Labour's ridiculous rules say it has to be someone Polish. But they can't complain because there's a freeze on jobs and they could be the next victim of natural wastage. Labour wants them to sacrifice their jobs for life and go fight for custom in chambers. But they're already working harder than they used to because the junior doctors do less.

Many consultants are also managers. Most doctors have no management training at all. Hardly a recipe for success. But they get sucked into implementing Labour's targets, even if they don't agree with them. There's no room for common sense in the system because the penalties for failure are draconian.

And they're knackered. Patient expectation, political pressure and litigation show no signs of pausing for breath. Waiting times must come down further, even though ITU is short of nurses and most of the beds are taken up by 85-year-olds who've been there for months, having the life slowly sucked out of them at huge expense. But you dare not question it. You mustn't give anyone the excuse to suspend you. We may have a whistleblowers' Act but the NHS is still run on fear.

Hospitals are going to be downsized, casualty departments are for the chop, work is being shifted out into the community and more and more junior doctors are fighting for fewer jobs. It's going to be tough enough holding on to yours for long enough to maximise the pension. Better not complain too much, certainly not in public. Thank Christ we've still got the common room to whinge in.

Medical Students

Medical schools have apparently been saved by women. If it was just down to academic achievement, they'd be all-female. And they can drink more than the blokes too. But have the attitudes changed since I was a girl?

I went down to my old medical school – it's now Guy's-King's-Thomas's-Poland – a vast expanse of students who never get to know each other or their teachers. Great for morale. So how do they welcome the freshers? Yes, it's a lard-eating competition. Down in Guy's bar, they put down a huge black plastic sheet, dentist's chair in the middle and force-feed the new recruits lard until they vomit. Who cares? You'll probably never see them again.

One student took freshers down to Cornwall on a hockey tour and made them drink a Bloody Mary made of their own blood. Quadruple vodka, drip in the arm, top it up with O-neg and skull it. He was disciplined for the misappropriation of NHS drips, not for making students drink their own blood. Still, it's progress, of a sort.

Maybe this is just a London, ex-public-school thing. Or maybe not. I was a lecturer in Birmingham, where the turning-out parade consisted of a competition, with T-shirts for the winners, to find the Slag of the Year, the Most Irritating Christian of the Year and the Person Likeliest to Have the Ugliest Children.

At Edinburgh, I was invited back to the Royal Medical Society, a social club for medical students. There was a baby in a pot in the middle of the bar.

'What's that?'

'It's a baby in a pot.'

'Yes but what's it doing in the bar?'

'I don't know. I haven't done obstetrics yet.'

The room was full of body parts. Doctors-to-be still like to think of themselves as a tribe apart, unreconstructed and unshockable.

Juniors

In 1989, I stood on stage whingeing about working 120 hours a week. Now they whinge about not doing enough. We used to learn by cutting up dead patients and killing live ones. Now they learn anatomy on plastic models and don't get any cutting at all. European law limits their hours, more students are being trained without enough training places, and nurses are taking over the world. For the first time in the history of the NHS, medical unemployment is a reality. And when you're feeling insecure about your job and suicidal to boot, you're not going to take on the system. Which is precisely what Labour wants.

In the old days, the learning curve was steep, you made your mistakes but if you survived, you had some experience and a team around you. Now no one on the front line has much experience or support. During the day, you're doing urology. At night, you're covering urology, orthopaedics, vascular surgery and ENT. On your own. You haven't really got a clue what you're doing so you just firefight until the next shift-worker comes on. You're forced to pay lip service to quality and safety and you'll still be halfway up the learning curve at the end of the job. You have no life and neither do some of your patients.

Some junior doctors, like the stout folk of Remedy UK, have enough fire in their bellies to save the NHS but it's hard to fight when you're always moving round and never sure where you'll end up next. Which is why managers and the BMA can fob you off so easily. And you don't want to be branded a troublemaker by anyone who might be writing your reference.

Bring Back Matron

The Tories wanted to bring back Matron, so Labour has to trump them. They want to bring back modern Matron. What are they going to do? Put her on wheels?

But maybe nurses can save the NHS. In America, the most litigious country of all, nurses do pretty much everything a doctor does. Diagnosis, surgery, anaesthesia, complex disease management, drinking too much and urinating in the flower bed. Could they do it over here?

The advantage of training nurses over junior doctors is that nurses often stay put whereas junior doctors move. So the hospital benefits more from its investment. But is there anything a doctor does that a properly trained nurse couldn't do just as well? Let's have a show of hands . . . Pretty much fifty-fifty, doctors and nurses, with patients abstaining.

If nurses do the same jobs as doctors, won't they want the same pay? There is the odd East End practice where all the staff get equal pay, even the receptionist, but they do have recruitment problems (except for receptionists). Generally doctors prefer earning five times more than nurses, even if the nurses manage all the chronic illnesses, do the same-day emergency appointments, knock off the vaccination and contraception and hit all the targets.

When I was a house officer, we did the killing and nurses did the caring. If you were lucky, they'd make you a nice cup of tea. If you were desperate, you'd make them one. And if you were an arsehole, they'd phone you up at three o'clock in the morning and ask you to write up temazepam for a patient who was asleep.

Then, in the year 2K, there was a cultural earthquake. Nurses could prescribe paracetamol without first clearing it with a doctor. There weren't many of them but the very notion that experienced professionals could dish out a tablet sold in thousands of corner shops across the land represented a giant leap forward for the nursing establishment and a wake-up call to the medical one.

Now there are nurses who can prescribe anything we can (or, at least, anything the PCT says we can). Doctors still have a certain snob value and better indemnity insurance. If you want to play doctors, you've got to take risks and accept the shit when it happens. So you need insurance. And a pay rise to cover it.

The cultural stereotypes of hard-drinking, gung-ho doctors doing operations they've never heard of with the book open on the table and timid nurses who aren't allowed to breathe until another nurse checks it first are very deep-rooted. Hence some doctors are still passing their arrogant incompetence on to patients, and many nurses still haven't crossed the paracetamol barrier.

Some, however, have gone way beyond it. When Sister Valerie Tomlinson famously whipped out a Cornish appendix we all got in a terrible froth but nurses have been dabbling illicitly with the instruments for years, usually to rescue cack-handed junior doctors. If it hadn't been for nurses helping me out on the special care unit, I'd be the UK's biggest baby killer. They put all the drips, drains and tubes in, I made the tea and took all the credit.

If we started from scratch, I'm not sure we'd reinvent doctors and nurses but we're stuck with the petty inter-professional rivalries now. If you split medicine up into lots of individual tasks, I'm sure nurses can do most of what a doctor does as well, if not better. But lots of patients are old, fat, depressed, demented, arthritic, anginal, bronchitic and very sick. And that's just the top half. Many need a generalist with wisdom, intellect and experience to sort them out. That's what I want when I'm finally dragged kicking and screaming onto an NHS ward. But we don't train them any more.

Medicine is being split up into tasks not just so people other than (and cheaper than) doctors can do it but also so organisations other than the NHS can bid for them. Privately run health centres and hospitals may in future be staffed by everyone bar a doctor. Which worries me slightly. I have no issue with nurses doing my surgery or giving my anaesthetic. If they're supervised by someone who knows what to do if shit happens. Because when doctors are patients, it always does.

Nurses, junior doctors and everyone working in all those Cinderella specialties are the future of the NHS. They might even save it, if enough money and time are given over to training, supervision and job creation. But that's long term, so it doesn't interest politicians. Well, not at the moment. It will in twenty years when we're all sick.

GPs

When I started my training scheme in 1988, everyone wanted to be a GP. By 2002, no one did. The government tried to recruit another 2,000 GPs but only managed three. And two have committed suicide.

General practice was unpopular because it's almost impossible to do well. You can't be a six-minute expert in every condition, have twenty-four-hour responsibility for your increasingly expectant patients and deal with the mountain of government targets. If I had to do that full-time, I'd either pretend to do everything that was expected of me, or I'd top myself. So I only do a day a week.

Anyone who survives general practice long enough to become a senior partner deserves a medal. I worked with one who finished a seventy-two-hour weekend shift, marched into the waiting room and stuck up a home-made health promotion poster: 'If you've got flu, fuck off.'

Not terribly New Labour but worth a try.

Another senior GP used to summon patients over the intercom: 'Come on, Mrs Jones, you big jelly-belly. Get your great flabby arse in here.' Not so funny when it's read out in court but who cares if you're retiring next week?

Morale is still at an all-time low, despite the pay rise, but then it always is. I've only ever twice seen really happy doctors. Once was in Jersey, which isn't in the NHS and lends itself to a life of uncontrolled hedonism (at least until medical students from Nottingham brought in an incurable strain of genital warts). The other was the GPs who got into fundholding.

I wasn't a fan of fundholding when Fat Ken Clarke brought it in. I was working in a practice that wasn't big enough to qualify for the scheme, and it didn't seem fair that fundholders could make a small fortune by cutting their prescribing costs and then keep the profits. They negotiated better deals for surgery, physio, investigations and outpatients when everyone else's money had run out in December. Treatment was no longer according to clinical need; it all depended on whether your notes had a GPFH stamp on them.

The GPs who jumped at the chance of fundholding loved it. They got a break from their patients to sharpen those entrepreneurial skills and transfer a bit of power from bloated, expensive, inefficient hospitals into general practice. They bought their own minibuses to ferry patients to and from outpatients and the family around Europe in the holidays. If you're going to have a market system, at least let the front-line staff control it.

General practices are small businesses and have more management skills and better computer systems that the rest of the NHS, which isn't saying a lot. As fundholding grew, practices pooled their budgets to form multi-funds which had more clout and represented larger groups of patients. The Stalinist limpet was in danger of being loosened.

Then Labour came in, hated fundholding on principle, shut it down and lost all the goodwill, expertise and energy of the GPs who'd built it up. Now Labour's done a U-turn and wants to give GPs commissioning power again. But they aren't nearly as enthusiastic to get their fingers burned again. And they don't need the money.

To solve the recruitment crisis, the BMA somehow negotiated a new contract with the government that allowed GPs to opt out of night duty and earn a lot of money by either hitting lots of targets or at least seeming to hit them. We'll never know if this represents good value or makes a big difference to patients because there wasn't a proper controlled trial comparing GPs practising as old-fashioned professionals to today's overstressed box-ticking puppets.

Having taken the money, GPs are supposed to feel indebted to the government and join in with a cunning plan to bankrupt their local hospitals by transferring all their work into the community. The GP with a special interest in, say, diabetes, will see most of the patients who previously fagged up to hospital. Fine so long as the hospitals service doesn't fold and there is still an expert somewhere to sort out the difficult diabetic with eight other diagnoses on forty tablets a day.

Most GPs are generalists at heart but worry that they are becoming deskilled, less employable and too expensive for the NHS. In many practices, it's easier to get an appointment with a doctor than with the practice nurse. I often end up doing the therapeutic gossip that the nurse used to do before she became a slave to the computer. I don't mind at all but I'm not sure I'll have a job in five years' time unless I specialise – in therapeutic gossip.

Surprise! The NHS Isn't 100 Per Cent British

The NHS was built on a tide of post-war optimism, so we think of it as quintessentially British. But the staff never have been. Nearly half the doctors and a quarter of the nurses registered to work in the NHS qualified overseas. They've propped up the NHS since its inception, working in areas shunned by British graduates, in single-handed GP practices in the most deprived areas or dead-end hospital jobs with no chance of career progression.

We steal medical staff from African and Asian countries where the life expectancy is barely half ours, and treat them like shit. They must be amazed at how much we whinge. Try picking bits of dead baby out of the rubble before you complain about the car parking.

Why Do Doctors Make Mistakes? Because We Can

The NHS, in common with all health systems, harms a lot of its customers. But excusing it with 'They were sick anyway. We've all got to die sometime' just won't wash in the twenty-first century. Every year we kill people with exactly the same errors.

Putting anti-cancer drugs into the spine rather than the vein, or vice versa. And still no one designs a syringe that only fits one or the other.

You become a doctor at twenty-three and have huge responsibilities. You wouldn't be allowed to fly a jumbo jet so young but then death in the air is a commercial disaster. Death in the NHS is cost-effective, if you can hide it from the lawyers. Pilots have to take time off for sleep, they're always under observation, they have to do everything in duplicate, they follow protocols, they have random breath testing and they have to have regular competency checks. Doctors just do it.

But we are at least trying to learn from the bad shit. Staff are now encouraged to come clean over their cock-ups. An amnesty that allows us to own up in a spirit of openness, without fear of humiliation and litigation. So, hands up who wants to kick us off? It won't leave this building, trust me.

Part of the problem is that the NHS is so slack, we don't even know when we've made mistakes. One senior partner summed up his forty years as a GP with 'Saved two, killed one . . . No, actually it was the other way round.'

When patients don't come back and see me, I don't know if I've killed you, cured you or you've quit in disgust. Just so long as you don't come back. My hero was a surgeon called Lord who developed a technique called the Lord's Stretch – not to be confused with the Lord's Prayer – for helping people who found it hard to pass motions. He stuck ten fingers up their arse. And stretched. Bugger me if they didn't come back. They must be cured.

'Whoops, Potassium' – My Mistake, No. 1

Hospital medicine is more immediate and you tend to remember your mistakes, especially if you're paid to. My first was in 1985, as a medical student, when I flushed a drip through with heart-stopping potassium rather than saline. I'd confused two identical ampoules, stored next to each other on a dimly lit shelf at three in the morning. Who's done that? Four of us. Fortunately I was so crap, the drip wasn't in properly.

Seventeen years later, the National Patient Safety Agency (NPSA) realised hundreds have died from mistaken potassium. From now, it's going to be locked away with the controlled drugs, and would I like to go on the six o'clock news to talk about my ordeal? So I entered into the spirit of openness, to help stop the carnage. I get home and my kids are playing doctors and nurses. Well, a new version: killer doctors and nurses.

But it's not human nature to cough to things. If you whizz past a speed camera and it doesn't flash, you tend not to shop yourself. The NPSA relies on a voluntary error reporting system. Very few GPs use it and only some hospital staff. A mate of mine was cauterising some anal skin tags – enjoy your Cornetto – and instead of lignocaine anaesthetic, the nurse squirted on an alcohol-based spray. This bloke's arse went *whoof!* like a Christmas pudding. Rather than admit the error, the doctor pretended it was part of the treatment, like a bedside flambé.

'Oh yes, here we go, crêpe Suzette. Can I have some Flamazine please, nurse?' And he got away with it. Said it was his first case of arse-on.

'It's Probably Not a Virus' – My Mistake, No. 431

In general practice, mistakes tend to be sins of omission. You fail to visit or you fail to make the diagnosis. Here's a letter I got seventeen years ago that still brings me out in a sweat:

Dear Dr Hammond,

I am deeply hurt about you making a mistake about my late husband's illness. You were very wrong about the virus. I am afraid it was more than that, and it killed him in the end. What you should have done is given him a thoroughly good examination and he might have been alive today. I've only just found out from the hospital that he had cancer and it was spreading all over his body. I shall never forget this mistake you made.

Yours faithfully . . .

It arrived halfway through my GP trainee year and in between patients. It was tucked tactfully between my coffee and HobNobs but it was already opened and round the health centre.

'You'll never guess what Gingerballs has gone and done.' Had I really told a man with terminal cancer 'It's probably a virus'? Lots of people do that, don't they? It's almost normal practice.

At least the letter ended with 'Yours faithfully'. A glimmer of hope? Maybe I wouldn't be sued if I got my apology in quick. I strolled out to reception and casually asked for the notes. They were already in my tray, with a Post-it note from Brian, my trainer, on the front.

'Read your last entry and see me later, you twat.'

I'd only seen the man once but the last entry was definitely my writing, so there was no getting out of it. In my usual effusive style, I'd written 'D&V, Abd. NAD, Prob. Viral. Adv.' So, he had diarrhoea and vomiting, I'd poked his stomach and given him some sort of advice about viruses. I couldn't see that standing up in court.

There was also a letter from a hospital in Cyprus which said he'd collapsed on holiday, was admitted as an emergency, found to have a melanoma on his back and died shortly afterwards. I couldn't quite tie it in with the diarrhoea and vomiting but I had vague memories of telling a pleasant elderly man to go off and enjoy his holiday and come back and see me if it hadn't settled when he got home. I might even have said, 'Go on, it'll do you the world of good.' Shit.

Brian was vaguely reassuring. The cancer was sure to have spread by the time I saw him and he was better off spending his last few days on a beach in Cyprus than under a scalpel in Swindon. I also phoned the Medical Defence Union, who advised me to arrange a meeting with the wife to talk about it. To my alarm, she accepted.

I still feel guilty – not about missing the diagnosis but about my preoccupation with covering my arse when here was a woman who'd suddenly lost her partner of nearly fifty years. She came alone, accepted my apology with quiet dignity and I never heard from her again.

I felt awful afterwards. For a month, I practised very defensive medicine, strip-searching every patient with so much as a sniffle and writing copious notes. Until Brian asked me to cut down because I was causing filing problems. But the penny had finally dropped that being a GP is a lot harder than I thought it was.

You can get a bit blasé about it when a lot of what you see is self-limiting illness but there's a fair bit out there that isn't 'probably a virus' and a lot of complex medical problems wrapped up in even more complex psychosocial problems that you haven't got a hope in hell of unravelling in under ten minutes. And as for all that uncertainty ... It's one of the hardest jobs in the world to do well. Which is why I tried a spell in the clap clinic. Yep, you can't go far wrong with knob-swabbing (well, you can but you're very unlikely to kill anyone). Oh but the smell, the smell.

Lawyers
The NHS loses billions each year either preparing for or fighting litigation.

The only place for a lawyer in hospital is in a bed. Or

perhaps a pot. Certainly not behind a big advertisement in casualty saying 'Has your doctor cocked up? Phone me now, no win, no fee.'

Virginia Bottomley described complaints as 'jewels' but some are 100-carat crap. A doctor who'd successfully managed shoulder dystocia (an obstetric emergency when the baby's shoulders get stuck, risking death from asphyxia) received a complaint because he sweated too much when delivering the baby.

At the other end of the spectrum are the Kohinoor complaints. 'Whoops, wrong kidney', that sort of thing. A woman was diagnosed with glaucoma and operated on. It was then discovered she didn't have glaucoma. She spent seventeen years and £30,000 trying to get an apology. As my consultant used to say, 'You've either got to be very rich or very stupid to sue the NHS.' Take on the Limpet and watch your life disappear in court.

I'm not a believer in no-fault compensation – we have to be accountable as individuals – but we also need safe systems to work in. When things go pear-shaped in hospital, you can trace the chaos right down the line. Example:

The patient, Mr J, was admitted for a routine hernia repair but the surgical ward was full because of the four-hour casualty time target, the six-month waiting list initiative and the pile-up on the ring road. Mr J was sent to the gynaecology ward where there was a space on the list because they'd cancelled a woman, Mrs M, due for hysterectomy. She'd been given a biscuit by the League of Friends volunteer and couldn't have her anaesthetic. Nobody told the gynaecologist so he spent four hours hunting for the bloke's womb before he chanced his arm and removed the bladder. The nurse didn't say anything because she's from the Philippines and apparently the words for 'uterus' and 'bladder' are very similar. And the anaesthetist didn't raise the alarm because she was asleep, having spent all night trying to sort out the pile-up on the ring road.

So, who's to blame? Mr J's lawyer would sue everyone, starting with the bloke who baked the biscuit, and it would take fifteen years and several million to reach court. What we need is a pool of money for swift and reasonable compensation for damage, whatever the cause. Then a swift and independent investigation into the cause. It doesn't need a dozen more quangos. Sort it out locally and quickly. Without lawyers, if possible. If you sue the NHS, all you do is deprive it of money. In effect, you're suing yourself. And it can only make the service worse.

What Sort of Money Are We Talking?

One of the joys of being a doctor is forking out thousands a year for professional indemnity insurance and then finding out how your money's been spent from the quarterly *Cautionary Tales* booklet. An anaesthetist was recently accused of 'harassing' a pregnant woman about her smoking. The woman delayed her Caesarean section by nipping out for a fag and then coughing so hard it made it hard to put the epidural in. Cue one grumpy anaesthetist:

'You've seen your daughter born. If you give up smoking you might see her get married too.' Not terribly tactful. But how much was the case settled for? Yes, £44,500 plus costs.

In the same month, a woman with bipolar disorder on lithium failed to have her levels monitored for twelve years and a prescription for a contraindicated diuretic tipped her into lithium toxicity. She saw one doctor with the shakes and constipation, who gave her diazepam, and another doctor was called in when she became confused and could not stand. He arranged a psychiatric appointment in two months. Her husband then took her to hospital, where the diagnosis was made. She was in a coma for forty-three weeks, suffered neurological impairment, memory loss and slurred speech. Her claim was settled for £28,000. The difference in the settlements (£44K for abruptness, £28K for poisoning) may have been down to the difference in the patients. One was private, the other wasn't. God bless the NHS.

Hit Me, I'm a Doctor

We all make mistakes. We should be accountable. We shouldn't be hit. If we want to save the NHS, we have to stop taking it out on the staff.

I've only been hit twice professionally. As a student, I was cuffed by a surgeon for not knowing the nerve that runs alongside the carotid artery (the vagus, since you ask). My revenge was to steal his brogues from the changing room and wear them on every ward round for the next eight weeks.

As a doctor, I was punched in 1988. I didn't see it coming and it landed plumb on the middle of my chin. It was in the middle of a busy ward and with plenty of witnesses but they all laughed. The aggressor was seventy-five and female, and didn't quite pack enough power to floor me. She was the wife of a diabetic man who'd fallen over after an early morning hypo. I cut his evening insulin and his sugar went the other way, causing him to fall over again. All my fault.

I've had a few disturbed patients to deal with in the clap clinic but as yet I've escaped the fate of my consultant, who bears an eight-inch facial scar from a machete attack. A survey of 4,000 GPs found that three quarters had faced a violent patient at least once and more than half had been physically assaulted. Stanley knife, a crowbar, a brick, a crutch, an electric fire, a beer glass . . . they should do a *Generation Game* special.

So what do you do? A tiny Birmingham GP hired a 6ft 2in, 14-stone Russian Sombo wrestling champion, to accompany him on visits where 'a white middle-aged middle-class doctor stands out like a walking cash-machine'. The rest of us now have to go on aggression management courses. In my role-play,

I was trapped in my chair with my lapel being ripped to shreds. But I was taught a cunning holding technique which involved grabbing and twisting the arm, and then applying unnatural forward pressure over the elbow joint until the patient agreed to behave.

As she was only 5ft 4in, I felt very unnatural pinning her down in a half nelson. Has family medicine really come to this? However many courses I go on, I doubt I'll ever learn to switch from 'How can I help you?' mode to 'I'm going to have to break your arm if you don't stop that' mode. How can I respond to your emotional needs when I'm scraping my heel down your shin?

In Praise of Receptionists

What you really need to survive in today's NHS is more receptionists. They're badly paid, poorly trained and vilified in the press. But without them the service would be on its knees.

Receptionists take the stick that patients wouldn't dare give the doctor, and yet many GPs are unaware of what goes on out the front of shop. Once, when surgery was running half an hour late, I saw a female patient march up to the counter and yell, 'Why doesn't Dr Morris get a fucking move on?' Remaining completely calm and in control, the receptionist picked up the phone and said, 'Dr Morris? Mrs Jenkins says, "Why don't you get a fucking move on?"' Now that's how to handle aggression and educate the GP at the same time. Pay them treble, I say.

Save the Staff

I once stood for Parliament – big mistake – in 1992. The Struck Off and Die Junior Doctors Alliance, SODJA, took eighty-seven votes off the Health Secretary William Waldegrave in Bristol West. A mandate to govern. We were trying to highlight the dangerous working conditions of junior doctors but I fear we lacked gravitas. Having an ice-cream van as a campaign vehicle didn't help. Neither did driving it around Clifton shouting 'What do we want? Willie Out! When do we want it? Now! . . . Willie, Willie, Willie . . . Out! Out! Out!'

I didn't realise you could make a speech at the count, however unelectable you were, until I was called up. I said, 'If you want a better health service, start by looking after the people working in it.' I don't mean paying us loads. If you work in the NHS, you don't do it for the money. Paying enough to cover the rent near where you work would be good. But what worries me most is the mental health of NHS staff.

If you can never do what's expected of you then, in time, your brain explodes. The NHS excels at killing the staff. Blair or Brown promises to turn around the NHS in time for the next election, and all the pressure gets passed down through the system. The lower you are down the tree, the less control you have and the worse you feel. The mental health of overseas NHS staff, stuck on the bottom rung and separated from what's left of their families, is a major concern. Or at least it should be. But they're not British. So we don't really care.

If politicians agreed their reforms with the staff and paced them sensibly, they could then trust the staff to deliver without stalking them with clipboards. Not rocket science and far fewer breakdowns all round. Instead, I get sent an NHS stress survey, to see how close to the edge I am. Fourteen pages, so very stressful filling it in. Page 13, question 327, they finally get to the point: 'Have you recently thought of the possibility of making away with yourself?' What are they talking here, masturbation or suicide? The difference between every day and never could really stuff up their statistics. I think I'll leave it blank.

Bring Back the Hospital Show
There are a number of key indicators of the health of the NHS: job turnover, staff suicides, the number of turds on the floor of

the urgent admissions' ward that the nurses step over while pretending not to notice. But by far the most important is Christmas Show Density.

In a happy hospital, porters, nurses, managers, domestics, doctors, receptionists and mortuary technicians join hands on stage (and wash them afterwards) to celebrate their work, personalities and culture. Yes, everyone remembers their first hospital show. Mine was 'Back Passage to India'. Or it could have been 'Room with a Poo', 'Flush Gordon' or 'On Her Majesty's Secret Cervix'.

In between the knob gags, you might even find a trickle of satire. In Taunton, they reworked Abba's 'Super Trooper' to 'Super Dooper (I'm in BUPA)'. And it's perhaps the only time of the year when staff from all disciplines function as a team. Every night sells out, the audience is implausibly enthusiastic, at least one consultant exposes himself during the balloon dance and all the proceeds go to the hospital charity (buying pillows for the intensive care unit).

Considering what a morale booster it is, you'd have thought every hospital would have one but very few do. When you're £20 million in debt, half the wards are closed, 200 staff are facing the chop and the rest are on sick leave, you just can't find a chorus line. And now staff work in shifts, rather than teams, nobody knows or sees each other.

Let's bring back the hospital show. Make it compulsory, open it to the public and bung in a few quality targets (hairiness of the dancing girls, slander of dodgy surgeons, number of impromptu consultations in the toilets).

Come On In

The NHS is always short staffed but training doctors takes time and money. So let's invent some. The British record goes to a Bradford man who impersonated a GP for thirty years before he was caught. And he was one of the good ones. He prescribed shampoo for conjunctivitis and creosote for a sore throat but he passed an appraisal and his patients didn't complain. Had he not been shopped by a member of his family he could still be practising. A few of the local pharmacists had their doubts but when the creosote sales are going so well, you don't like to complain.

Dr Bogus hailed from Pakistan, where he'd worked as a compounder: an unqualified chemist who treats common ailments with his own remedies, such as Day Creosote and Night Creosote. He fooled the GMC with a fake medical degree and reference. Other bogus doctors have forged certificates of registration to waft under the noses of desperate employers. In one celebrated case, a dyslexic man typed his own certificate, Tippexed out all the mistakes and corrected them in biro. This proved to be the passport to a brilliant career.

Without a single O-level to his name, he started out as a casualty officer on the south coast and then decided on a career in anaesthetics, pumping knockout drugs into babies and old ladies until he was finally apprehended for insurance fraud. His consultant described him as 'by no means the worst anaesthetist I've worked with'.

Anyone in the audience who isn't yet a doctor can be by the end of the interval. There are some fake qualifications by the bar nuts and a pile of white coats in the bogs. Enjoy yourselves. The NHS is so vast and unaccountable, nobody will ever track you down. And it's great if you need to lie low for a while. As I was saying to Dr bin Laden, only the other day.[1] Lovely man, great big hands. Probably shouldn't put him in charge though.

See you in half an hour.

---

[1] When I first made that gag in 2002, it was considered amusing. Now it's prophetically unfunny. But not as tasteless as the observations of a Manchester anaesthetist: 'Eight foreign doctors – three bombs, no deaths. Harold Shipman – one syringe, three hundred deaths. Makes you almost proud to be British.'

GARETH

'Morning. Have a seat.'

'Haven't met you before.'

'I'm Dr Hammond. I only work Thursdays.'

'I don't want a doctor who only works Thursdays.'

'Dr Rose . . .'

'. . . is booked up for five weeks.'

'This is more to do with Dr Bethel. I've had an urgent call from him.'

'And?'

'He says that the reason you've had night sweats and coughed up a bit of blood is because you've got tuberculosis.'

'I know that.'

'You were discharged two weeks ago with instructions to return three times a week to have your drugs under supervision. And you've only been the once.'

'So?'

'So Dr Bethel's very worried.'

'He's not capable of emotion. Look into his eyes and he blanks you. There's nothing behind them.'

'Well, there must be something. He's editor of the *European Journal of Respiratory Physiology*.'

'Look. I don't like the man and I don't like his drugs. I got indigestion and my urine went red.'

'That's the rifampicin. You should have been warned about that.'

'My tears went red too. Freaked the dog out.'

'I thought dogs could only see in black and white.'

'Not strictly true. And they've got great night vision.'

'Anti-tuberculosis drugs are very powerful because they need to be. It's a very difficult disease to eradicate. The bug that causes it—'

'Bug?'

'*Mycobacterium tuberculosis*, has a thick cell wall with a large lipid content, which allows it to survive inside host cells and resist digestion by preventing phagosome–lysosome fusion.'

'You're reading that off the computer.'

'But the body's immune system keeps fighting, so you end up with a chronic T-cell-mediated inflammatory response, with the formation of granulomas where the mycobacteria can lie dormant for many years.'

'If they're dormant, why not let them be?'

'Yours aren't any more. They've reactivated. We call it post-primary TB.'

'Where did I get it?'

'Somewhere on your travels. Africa, India, Tower Hamlets. You could have had it for years. If I did chest X-rays on my elderly patients, a lot of them would show signs of old TB infection.'

'So you're treating all of them with piss-staining poison?'

'Their TB is inactive but yours is open. You could get seriously ill without treatment.'

'When I was in hospital, I felt like shit. That place has a serious karma problem. The walls are grey, there's no sunlight, there's no privacy, you can't get any sleep, the food's inedible and the staff are miserable as sin. And yes, I did think I might die. But since I've stopped taking the drugs and come home, I'm eating well, getting some sunlight and healing myself. And I feel much better already.'

'What do you mean, healing yourself?'

'Through meditation and prayer. Focusing the mind's capacity to heal the body. And then there's Mrs Linton. She's harnessing a healing energy and transmitting it through her to me.'

'And you believe her?'

'Yes, I do, actually. I can feel the energy running into me, like a warm sensation. And my aura feels much better after. I don't need your drugs.'

'A warm aura is fine but this is life and death. Active TB is highly infectious and you're putting others close to you at risk. So you have to take the tablets. You can be sectioned if you don't.'

'Really?'

'If you were a cow, you'd be put down. Remember Shambo?'

'Dr Hammond, can I ask you, have you ever had any communication skills training?'

'I've been a lecturer in communication skills at both Birmingham and Bristol medical schools, and in 1995 I won the prestigious Owen Wade Teacher of the Year Award.'

'Yes, but have you had any communication skills training?'

'No.'

'Mrs Linton could teach you a thing or two about acknowledgement. She's healing me now.'

'No, she isn't.'

'She can do it from a distance. I can feel her warmth flowing into me.'

'How far does her warmth travel?'

'As far as Mrs Linton likes. Currently, she's distance-healing George Bush, Gordon Brown and Osama bin Laden.'

'All at the same time?'

'Yes.'

'Look, if you're not going to take the drugs, will you at least come and see me next week?'

'Any day but Thursday.'

'Ah. Would you like a copy of my book?'

'No.'

'It's free.'

'All right then.'

RUBY

'Good morning. What can I do for you?'

'My husband's started washing himself in urine.'

'Is there anything else I can do for you?'

'No.'

'His own urine?'

'As far as I know.'

'And?'

'And nothing really. That's it. He shampoos in it, he dabs it on his face and he pours it up his nose with something that looks like a watering can.'

'Does he swallow it?'

'Well, I suppose you would swallow a bit if you poured it up your nose.'

'No, I mean does he drink it deliberately?'

'Why would he do that?'

'Lots of people do.'

'Says who?'

'Dr Google. In India, they've been doing it for five thousand years, in Japan for two thousand and the Romans and Greeks were into urine therapy long before Christ.'

'He didn't do it as well, did he?'

'Who knows? It's allegedly endorsed in the good book. "Drink waters out of thine own cistern and running waters out of thine own well." Proverbs 5:15–17.'

'Yes but what's the point?'

'Well, drinkers believe it improves general health and well-being, gives you energy and calms you down. Some even think that as your urine is formed, it picks up vital messages about your body's immune system and retains them.'

'And what do you think?'

'If you believe drinking your own pee will make you feel better then I'm sure it will. Think of it as homeopathy with attitude.'

'Yes, but won't it do you any harm?'

'If you go for a sterile midstream sample and limit yourself to a cup or two a day, it probably won't harm you.'

'And what does it taste like?'

'I've only ever tried it on St Thomas's Hospital rugby tour in Cornwall in 1984, and I can't quite recall.'

'Why?'

'Because it was a lager top, so I'm not sure what was urine and what was Heineken.'

'No, why did you drink it?'

'Oh, right. Have you ever played Commander Biddleebums?'

'No.'

'It's like Simon Says. But if you don't do what Commander Biddleebums says, then the punishment is much worse.'

'So Commander Biddleebums said, "Drink your own urine"?'

'That's it.'

'And St Thomas's Hospital sanctioned that sort of behaviour in 1984?'

'They didn't stop it. Drinking games reinforce the public-school model of medicine: the dean as head boy, the consultants as prefects and everyone else as a fag. You don't challenge the hierarchy, just shut up and do what you're told.'

'Until you become Commander Biddleebums?'

'Absolutely. I figured that out very quickly.'

'Do you know anyone who's drunk their own urine who isn't a medical student?'

'Yes. I know a woman who claims she can detect her diet from the taste of her urine. Apple crumble makes it sweet, for example.'

'And diabetes?'

'Absolutely. It used to be diagnosed by tasting.'

'Doesn't it make your breath stink?'

'Strangely not. She has honey-fresh breath and kisses with confidence. Does your husband's hair smell of wee?'

'Not so you'd notice.'

'Does it look clean?'

'Oh yes, it's got plenty of bounce.'

'Well, there you are then. No one's going to know and if they use the bathroom, they'll think it's baby shampoo.'

'So you don't think he'll stink the house out?'

'For some odd reason, people who wash in urine don't smell and neither do their houses. My friend says she gets more hugs when she bathes in it because her friends think she smells more "me-ish".'

'Is it true that it cures athlete's foot?'

'Possibly. Fresh urine contains urea, a moisturiser in many proprietary skin creams and is toxic to bacteria and fungi.'

'So it might work?'

'Well, Peter Tatchell swears by it, and so did my grandmother.'

'Anyone else?'

'Japanese POWs used urine compresses on war wounds and tropical ulcers, squaddies often pee in their boots to prevent foot root and bricklayers used to pee on their hands to prevent dermatitis from lime contact. Some claim their sinus and allergy problems have been cured by nasal washouts using a specially made Neti pot.'

'The watering can?'

'If you like. And in Germany, they've sold over two hundred and fifty thousand copies of the urophile's bible, *The Golden*

Fountain: The Complete Guide to Urine Therapy by Coen van der Kroon.'

'Do you know what my husband says? "Drink piss. A million swamis can't be wrong."'

'Charming. Would you like a hug?'

'No.'

'Have a photo of Des, then.'

'I thought he was cancer patients only.'

'Oh, I think you've earned it.'

89 MINUTES TO SAVE THE NHS
Part Two: Swimming Upstream

In at the Shallow End

My GP trainer Brian used to say, 'Life is a pool of shit and our job is to direct people to the shallow end.' Working in the NHS is like diving into a river of shit, pulling bodies out and trying to put them back together again. You get so knackered that you don't have time to wander upstream and look at who's pushing them in.

So let's walk up to the source and what do we find? A pub car park full of hypothermic, hypodermic smokers, drinking and drugging themselves into oblivion and eating salty lard. And safe and cosy behind the bar, the Chancellor. He loves all his regulars. Pay the tax on fags and booze and die before you put too much strain on the pension fund.

How can we save the NHS from coked-up, boozed-up, smoked-up lard buckets? Then again, should we try? Bad habits are what make us human. And if there were no drugs and alcohol, there'd be no comedy, no art, no literature, no music, no doctors. You can't be too hard on us.

Maybe the problem with the NHS is not that we're short staffed but that we've got too many patients. We need to go upstream to stop the logjam further down. We have the highest teenage pregnancy rate in Europe. One family planning expert recommended that all young girls be given contraceptive implants with their rubella booster. Who agrees with that? . . . Just you, sir. And what do you do? . . . You're an obstetrician.

Missing the Point

If all you've ever known is a cycle of sexual abuse, violence, criminality, drink, unemployment, family breakdown, heroin and despair, then no amount of fresh fruit and cholesterol checks are going to make you healthy. If your husband never lets you out of the house, you need more than a cervical smear. Politicians talk about the 'underclass' being 'hard to reach' but the smack, alcohol and tobacco industries seem to reach them very effectively.

A lot of health care misses the point. By the time you arrive at a GP's surgery or a casualty department, the damage has been done. You can't improve health from a box in a health centre or a hospital. As George Bernard Shaw put it, 'Take the utmost care to be well born.' Choosing your parents may be an intervention too far, and tinkering with genes is hotly debated. But we all need a good placenta. It's our lifeblood.

A bad placenta is bad news. If you don't die, it causes irreversible damage to your growth, development and intellect, and greatly increases your risk of future disease. We blather on about the dangers of passive smoking in pubs but smoking in pregnancy is manslaughter. Anyone caught doing it should be given a nicotine patch. Over the mouth. Sorry, I'm having a right-wing moment. You need a small hole for the folic acid supplements.

Folic Acid

Back in 1997, I argued that it was negligent not to fortify flour with folic acid to prevent neural tube defects (NTDs) like spina bifida. Ten years on and we still haven't. While the government dithers, 900 pregnancies a year are affected by spina bifida, a third of which result in termination. Half of these could be prevented. There is no ribbon for neural tube defects. And it's difficult to say. So we don't.

In spina bifida, the bones don't close round the spinal cord and the nerves can bulge out on the unborn baby's back and become damaged. This happens very early on in pregnancy – usually before you know you're pregnant. The evidence that folic acid can prevent this has been around since 1991, when the Medical Research Council's Vitamin Study Group showed the incidence of NTDs could be reduced by 75 per cent if all pregnant women took 400 micrograms each day from before conception to the end of the twelfth week of pregnancy.

Given that half of all pregnancies are unplanned, and only a third of people can remember to take tablets effectively, telling women to take daily folic acid supplements was never going to work. So what did the Tories do? Send out leaflets to GPs to remind women to take folic acid.

By 1996, only 9 per cent of UK women knew about folic acid. The US Centers for Disease Control recognised that health education and tablets would never deliver a significant reduction in NTDs, especially since their prevalence is greatest amongst the young and poor who don't plan pregnancies and are less aware of health issues. American food manufacturers were ordered to add folic acid to flour and a variety of staple foodstuffs as the only realistic chance of prevention. This came into effect from January 1998, and Canada and Chile followed suit. In these countries, there has been a 30–50 per cent drop in NTDs.

In the UK, only one in ten pregnant women gets enough folic acid. It's already added to many breads and cereals, and increasing the level in flour would not significantly mask vitamin B12 deficiency in the elderly, which is the main argument against. Since 1997, there have been 5,000 babies born with NTDs that could easily have been prevented, and 2,500 needless terminations. That's a lot of keepsake photos of dead babies that would be alive if we took public health seriously.

Fluoride

Bad teeth are as big a social and sexual turn-off as obesity. But they're far more preventable. If only we'd put enough fluoride in the water. There's a huge class divide in dental health. Some areas of the UK have six times the level of tooth decay than others. It's unsightly, painful and results in hundreds of thousands of avoidable anaesthetics and tooth extractions each year. One in five of Glasgow's and one in three of Liverpool's most deprived five-year-olds have had teeth pulled.

But in the inner-city areas of Newcastle and Birmingham, the level of tooth decay amongst children is lower than in some affluent areas of the UK. Why? Children in these areas belong to the select 10 per cent of the UK population that has a fluoride level in the water of one part per million. True, there is already fluoride in toothpaste but adding fluoride to the water has an additional benefit. Certainly in areas where tooth decay is rampant and tooth-brushing has yet to become a national pastime.

The case for adequate fluoridation in these areas is overwhelming. There is no good evidence of serious side-effects at this level and it could cut the level of caries in half.

Fluoride strengthens teeth enamel by improving its crystal formation, which in turn makes it more resistant to acid. It also slows down the demineralisation of mature teeth and the formation of plaque. It can occasionally stain the teeth but this is usually undetectable and doesn't affect their health. Rampant caries causes teeth that are horrible to look at, don't work properly, fall out and give you dog breath. Medicine is always swings and roundabouts but the government's refusal to protect the teeth of the poor is as good a way as any to keep them in their place. We'll never have enough NHS dentists. So why not start with fewer bad teeth?

Deaf Babies

There's a Native American dialect where the sounds of the words are so similar that unless you've been exposed to them in the first eighteen months of life, you'll never be able to hear the difference. The vast majority of the trillions of connections made in your brain occur during this time and are vitally dependent on a baby's ability to receive new sights and sounds. Perception is everything.

So it's vital that any baby who is born deaf is diagnosed as quickly as possible to prevent serious and long-term damage to language and communication. There are two hearing tests designed to pick up deafness in babies and children. One, called the otoacoustic emission test (OET), is cheap, easy to do and effective. The other, called a distraction test, isn't. Guess which one the NHS majored in?

The OET was discovered thirty years ago and it's simple to do. A small probe is placed in the sleeping baby's ear and sends a brief sound signal into the ear. In a healthy ear, the sound is reflected back like an echo from cells in the cochlea. These cells are vital to hearing and if they are damaged or abnormal, the echo is reduced or non-existent.

Like many medical advances, the inventor of OET, Professor David Kemp, took ten years to convince his colleagues that ears produce their own echo sound but good evidence has been around that OET works for years and in 1997, the Medical Research Council approved it. That same year, the Department of Health found that of the 840 children born each year with a significant hearing problem, only half were picked up by eighteen months, and a quarter were still undiagnosed at three and a half years of age. Over half of all babies born deaf suffer irreparable harm to their brain development because we fail to diagnose them. So why did it take until 2006 before OET was introduced as a screening test? Possibly because cochlear implants are expensive and deafness is just not sexy enough.

Smoking

People should be free to die young but two thirds of smokers at least want to try to stop. Only a fraction get the best treatment. But helping people quit is the single most useful thing a GP could do. We see smokers five times a year, we're paid to know who smokes and to give advice, there are treatments that work and patients want our help. So why are we so crap at giving it?

According to Dr Alex Bobak, most other GPs only refer a fraction of their patients to stop smoking services and give bad advice on how to stop. Sixty-three per cent of GPs don't offer any treatments, 61 per cent don't think the treatments work and 23 per cent don't think it's their job.

And it gets worse. Doctors aren't trained in smoking cessation. In one study 51 per cent of GPs thought nicotine caused cardiovascular disease, 49 per cent thought it caused strokes and 41 per cent thought it caused cancer. Six per cent thought nicotine replacement therapy was as harmful as cigarettes.

As for smokers, 62 per cent thought nicotine caused cardiovascular disease, 63 per cent thought it caused strokes and 71 per cent thought it caused cancer. Thirty-seven per cent thought nicotine replacement therapy was as harmful as cigarettes. So, marginally less well informed than GPs. (Nicotine is what you get addicted to, it's all the chemicals in tar that kill you.)

A good smoking cessation service gets 20 per cent of people off cigarettes in the long term. Half of all long-term smokers die prematurely from a smoking-related death. So you need to treat ten smokers to save one life.

Compare that to cholesterol-lowering drugs, where you have to treat 107 low-risk patients over five years to stop one death. You have to treat 700 people with mildly raised blood pressure for a year to prevent a single stroke, heart attack or death. And you have to screen 1,140 women over ten years to prevent one death from cervical cancer.

Smoking cessation is one of the most effective treatments around. Especially if you can save a placenta. GPs find it boring but receptionists, nurses and health-care assistants don't. They love it. And they're really good at it. There are now plenty of smoking cessation clinics that could take on far more smokers if only they came forward. The least doctors could do is show an interest and point people in the right direction.

Whatever Happened to Public Health?
Public health in the UK is a shambles. Obesity, smoking, sexually transmitted infections, work-related stress, alcohol-related illness and aggression, unwanted pregnancies, disability and mental illness. All on the rise. Other infectious diseases like TB and measles are coming back and vaccination levels are falling. The poverty levels in cities haven't budged since the fifties.

Public health is what's supposed to reduce inequality, keep us healthy and protect us from SARS or bird flu or dirty bombs or MMR scares. But the service is on its knees, largely due to the continuous 'redisorganisation' of the NHS. Health improvement is a slow-drip affair and you need a coherent, well-funded strategy over decades to achieve success, not lots of pissed-off staff constantly reapplying for their jobs.

Which is a pity. Over the last century, UK life expectancy increased by thirty years, mainly due to improvements in public health and the economy (housing, sanitation, employment) rather than wonder drugs. In the twenty-first century, we're self-destructing at one end, and going demented at the other. These are huge public health challenges that require solutions based on sound research, rather than knee-jerk political reform.

The destruction of public health may well be because of its challenge to the government. As one consultant put it:

To say that there must always be change and reform is to forget the fundamental public health questions of what is the evidence for it? And what will be the health impact? Right now, there is considerable evidence that successive reorganisations of the NHS have been wasteful of time, money and people, and have not delivered service improvement.

But if there's no public health service to improve public health, who's going to do it?

Plugging the Gap

Poor people get sick – always have done, always will. We have one of the most unequal 'civilised' societies and it's getting more unequal. The way to save the NHS is to tackle poverty, not pour money into hospitals. But how? Rolling out patient choice programmes and NICE guidelines from the centre is going to make bog-all difference to inequality. They're just more tools for the well-educated to play the system.

Maybe Alan 'Postie' Johnson can deliver a reverse postcode lottery in health care. We know the areas where shit happens every day, and where people die a decade early, so give them more resources. Instead of banning fat people and smokers from treatment, fast-track them before they get in such a state that nothing can be done. Intervene early, before that placenta shrivels.

Allocating limited resources is tough. Do you give them to patients who complain bitterly with less pathology, or those with advanced illness but a very stiff upper lip? Money for the elderly, quietly surviving in a state of hypothermic malnutrition? Or good behaviour incentives for crack addicts and gymslip mums?

The carers of the incurably sick offer unbelievable value for money, because we usually don't pay them. And those we do pay hardly have their buttocks in butter. People who work in care homes for those with severe learning difficulties or dementia get about £6 an hour. Many are unbelievably positive, loving and cheerful, given the nature of what they do. I get £60 an hour as a salaried GP and I'm not sure I offer ten times the value. I can certainly be ten times as grumpy.

Sure Start

SHAs are where the money needs to be – not strategic health authorities but 'shit happens areas'. I like the idea of Sure Start. Put children's centres smack in the middle of the most deprived areas, largely run by the mums, with the best advice on early education, family support, contraception, vaccination, smoking cessation and childcare. Get children sorted by the age of three, or it's too late.

Young mothers are the most depressed cohort of an increasingly depressed population. Give them help and support and they'll share ideas and be good parents without being branded failures or ordered what to do.

The problem is politics. Sure Start is expensive but, like any complex public health project, it'll take years to reap big benefits, building slowly, spreading by word of mouth, figuring out what works best and sharing it. Stop teenagers smoking now and there'll be a huge dip in heart disease in thirty years (which the government will attribute to its latest reforms). Sort out teenage contraception, and the reduction in crime and drug abuse will kick in fifteen to twenty years from now (entirely due to current policing levels).

Politics never waits. It demands results by the next conference. So you interfere and over-evaluate, like kids pulling up their radishes after a day to see if they're growing. Use the evidence to offer the best childcare, teaching and parental support. And let it grow. They've had it in Scandinavia for years and it works. Slowly.

We also need to free up the social workers to help the most deprived of the deprived who won't come to the centres. Placenta, perception, parenting. That's my mantra. Children need more stability than a twenty-eight-inch flat screen screwed to the wall. Or as Jack Dee put it, 'They say we should stop smacking our kids. Maybe we should stop fucking them first.'

Big Pharma

How influenced are we by the pharmaceutical industry? Much like doctors, drug company employees are largely conservative and try to help patients, preferably with drugs. A lot of these are fantastic, if only the NHS could afford them, but there'll always be the odd lethal weapon which they try to hide for as long as possible, and then they all get branded as evil. No trial is perfect, no drug is without risk, but the sooner you own up to a turkey, the less bird flu you pass on.

Just occasionally, a drug chief lets his guard down and says something of astonishing honesty. In 2003, Dr Allen Roses, a vice-president at GlaxoSmithKline, admitted that 'the vast majority of drugs – more than 90 per cent of them – only work in 30–50 per cent of patients'. Trouble is, he doesn't know which 30–50 per cent. Still, this rather stuffs the theory that all humans are essentially the same so we can all be lumped together in huge trials to find a drug that works for us.

There are plenty of patients who don't respond to a drug when the best evidence says they should, and this may be because there are as-yet-undiscovered genetic differences. Maybe GSK think they know how to market these. Why else would you admit to them? In the meantime, don't feel guilty if a drug doesn't work for you. And don't take it either.

Just as problematic is wanting to take a drug for something soul-destroying (Alzheimer's, cancer, arthritis, blindness) and being told the NHS (at least where you live) won't fund it. This may be because NICE says it doesn't work well enough or it's

not good value for money. Or it could be because your local
NHS is broke.

There are loads of these new drugs in the pipeline, and the
NHS won't fund them all. Labour promotes patient choice but
won't let you choose to top up your NHS treatment with
private drugs it won't fund, for fear of endorsing a two-tier
system. But there will always be those who can afford to pay
more. And if politicians aren't able to force drug companies to
cut their prices, the least they can do is let NHS patients get
them via the cheapest route. Preferably before they die.

The bottom line with drug companies is that they want us
to take their drugs. So paying their chief executives huge
bonuses and overpricing the drugs is a touch short-sighted,
even if it does cost billions to get a new product to market. In
India, the idiosyncratic patent laws allow cheap drug
production and a 'pharmacy for the Third World'. The UK
government is currently trying to renegotiate the tariff it pays
for drugs but, in America, Medicare is prohibited from
negotiating drug prices with manufacturers thanks to a dodgy
bill passed in the middle of the night on the back of some
obscenely lucrative political lobbying.

Big pharma can also use the media to throw out a huge
trawling net and drag us in. Drug company press releases get
parachuted into media scare stories with barely a word
changed. People don't go to the doctor now because they have
diseases but because they have risk factors. Or rather, they think
they might have a risk factor after reading the Tuesday health
supplement.

Whoever heard of female sexual dysfunction? Neither had I
until it was invented to sell pills. I looked at the criteria – have
you ever not felt like sex for a few days in the last month? – and
I've got female sexual dysfunction too. Anxiety's been upgraded
to social phobia, because it sounds more scary. You can't bear
people being around you. Most Australians have it, apparently.

Drug companies are victims of their own success. We've cracked most of the exciting diseases young people used to get and we're left with the ones you get with too many birthdays, the ones no one can cure. So we have to invent some. A GP I know has a T-shirt with 'CAMRA' written on it – the Campaign for Real Ailments – because all he ever sees is media-induced anxiety.

In America, they have direct consumer advertising. Every citizen is a potential pill-popper for every possible complaint. No longer do you use a doctor to get them either: you request your drug of choice from your 'prescriber'. One TV ad is for genital herpes. Well-off middle-class man in happy embrace with well-off middle-class woman: 'I have genital herpes.' Woman: 'I don't.' Man: 'Because I care.' Then a black couple, another white couple and a Hispanic couple. And then the name of the drug.

There are loads of ads for erectile dysfunction, with helpful warnings like: 'Please check with your prescriber if your erection lasts for more than four hours or you develop vision problems.' That sounds like a great sales pitch for teenage boys. And there's an extraordinary ad for Viagra to the tune of 'Viva Las Vegas'. Sing along now: 'Viva Viagra . . .'

The culture is pure consumerism. The consumer goes in to the prescriber to request the drug from the TV ad, and the prescriber feels compelled to prescribe, because otherwise the consumer takes his or her business next door to the next prescriber. I'm all for giving patients power and choice but I'd rather it was done on the basis of evidence than Elvis.

Trust Me, I'm *The Lancet*

Most of us don't believe all we read in the papers but what about esteemed medical journals like the *British Medical Journal* and *The Lancet*? This is where we go to find out if a drug really works or a health scare stacks up. So can we trust what we read? And are these journals any good at identifying medical fraud? No. Most journals don't even have procedures for dealing with misconduct or handling allegations of fraud. They're run by a few people in an office with some publishing software and a photocopier.

Many are largely in the pay of big pharma. They have few independent resources available to them and most journal editors work part-time. So we can't spot the cheats who harm patients and waste money to further their careers or up the share price. Half of what appears in even the best medical journals is probably bollocks. Trouble is, we don't know which half.

Medical journals are an extension of the pharmaceutical industry. The drug adverts they carry show their financial dependence on the industry but harder to spot is the bias of industry-sponsored randomised controlled trials. These are supposedly the highest form of evidence. A large trial published in a major journal gets global media coverage. If it comes up with the right answer, and it usually does, the drug companies milk this for all it's worth, spending a million dollars on reprints.

Amazingly (or not), studies funded by a company are four times more likely to have results favourable to the company than studies funded from other sources. So how do drug companies manage to get the results they want? Easy. You can conduct a trial of your drug against a treatment known to be inferior. Or trial your drugs against too low a dose of a competitor drug. Or use too high a dose (making the competitor seem toxic). You can use multiple endpoints and just publish the one that's favourable. Or do multi-centre trials and just publish the favourable centres, or even just publish a subgroup that seems to work.

Only drug companies have the resources to construct the really large trials that get into the top journals. So three quarters of the trials published in the major journals are funded by the industry. But if the industry doesn't fund this research, who will? Higher taxes for more publicly funded research – now there's a vote-winner.

When I blather on about nationalising the pharmaceutical industry, usually at drug company dinners, the audience punches me. We're good guys, we used to be doctors, we're so tightly regulated these days, we can't hide the bad stuff any more. This confuses me. Most of the doctors, politicians and journalists I meet seem good guys too. Even I seem like a good guy sometimes. But lump us all together in aggressive, profit-driven, win-at-all-costs organisations and we don't all behave like good guys.

At the very least, there should be a legal requirement to publish all clinical trials, no matter how crap or corrupted they are, or how disappointing the findings, so we get the whole picture.

Perhaps drug companies could pay into a huge research and training fund so researchers could do their stuff without an individual company breathing down their backs and doctors could enjoy their training without having their buttocks tattooed by Glaxo. Or maybe doctors could pay for their own education. Or maybe monkeys will fly out of my Glaxo-tattooed butt.

Marketing

Here's a typical consultation for me:

'Your chest does sound a bit mucky . . . It's probably a virus.'

'I want antibiotics.'

'I'm not giving them to you.'

'I'm not leaving.'

'I'm not budging.'

'I know the route your children take to school.'

'Are you allergic to amoxycillin?'

'Can't I have Distaclor?'

'Why?'

'Because it's written on your stethoscope.'

And my tongue depressors. And my pens. And my pads. And my coffee mug. And my phone card. I could go on but you get the picture. When it comes to drug companies advertising in the surgery, there's a lot of it about. Doctors pick up a plethora of promotional freebies every time the drug rep calls. I get most of mine on the medical cabaret circuit, in the pretence of using them for props, but they have an uncanny knack of resurfacing in my consultations. In the heat of the moment, you put on the first rubber glove you can find, even if it does sport the name of the nation's favourite haemorrhoid cream.

So does all this subliminal brain manipulation divert doctors from the path of rational prescribing to what's written on their pens? None of us would admit it but then drug companies wouldn't persist in ploughing money into freebies if it didn't. Today's freebies are pretty limp – none of them would look out of place in an 'everything under a pound' shop – but older doctors tell of trips abroad, Turkish baths and tickets to Twickenham. And who can forget those two 'leading-edge female presenters', upstairs in that dodgy East End pub?

Then there are the free gifts. Over the years, I've been given six saws to cut through my seat belt in an emergency (three with accompanying hammer to break the window), one 'health promotion shower gel' with 'Now Examine Your Testicles' written on the side, four sets of chattering teeth to advertise an arthritis drug, a phallic fan, four rape alarms and seven squeezy balls that are either stress relievers or prosthetic testicles. And a Stanley knife (for opening letters, apparently).

A rep promoting a thrush cream gave me two toothbrushes, perhaps thrush brushes, with an emergency triangle, presumably so you can put it outside your door and let the world know you've got the itch. She also gave me an emergency jacket and torch. Then the penny dropped. You're driving along the M4 at midnight and get a bad case of the itch. So you pull over, put on your jacket, put up your triangle and brush yourself on the verge, guided by your torch.

Another promoting an antidepressant 'that won't affect your sex life' gave me a pair of tweezers, presumably to help you find the penis that made you so depressed in the first place. By contrast, the Prozac rep gave me a desk toy which looks suspiciously like a turd floating in a sea of bile and makes me quite moody just to look at it. But it's got a one-way clock that only the GP can see. After six minutes, you tell them to piss off and give them some Prozac. Very subtle, subliminal advertising. There are even Prozac sweeties (much cheaper than the real thing and almost as effective).

Then there's Cipramil, an antidepressant sold to me with a fluffy chick with a squint in a baseball cap. Just as I was trying to figure out the connection with depression, out popped a toy car with 'Cipramil' written on it. Look closely and you might spot a hose connecting the exhaust to the driver's window. But my favourite gift ever was from the rep selling drugs for Parkinson's disease. Three juggling balls. Less of a toy, more of a diagnostic tool.

It's tightened up a bit now. The piss-up has been replaced by the Post-it note and any activity that could not remotely be described as educational has to be paid for in person. Not all doctors see reps but even those who feel they can live without a bastardised barley sugar can't escape the hype. For every pound the government spends supplying doctors with rational prescribing information based on the best available scientific evidence, the drug industry spends fifty. Aside from all the mailshots that go directly towards recycling, at least half of our magazines are taken up by drug ads.

There are Femidoms stapled to the front page (rather defeating their purpose), free pieces of sandpaper to help male doctors experience the discomfort of thrush and photos of women shaving ('Don't treat her like a man'). My all-time most tasteless ad was a treatment for heavy periods, which featured a woman swimming above a circling shark.

Packaging

And let's not forget the packaging. One brand of HRT, Kliofem, was launched with a vanity tablet holder. Extensive market research apparently found that some women find the idea of taking HRT stigmatising and worry about leaving it around the house lest the cleaner should spot it.

Just the sight of the famous blue Viagra diamond can give men an erection. I know men who keep one on the bedside cabinet, just in case. Just knowing it's there does wonders for performance anxiety. However, it's so recognisable, you really might want to hide it in a vanity case. Especially if you're having an affair. There are other drugs that do the job just as well but come in a much more discreet muddy beige.

Before tablets for erectile dysfunction, the most effective treatment was a change of partner. However, it's got unpleasant side-effects and isn't available on the NHS. We used to be able to prescribe Christmas puddings, which are the next best thing, but no more. Shame. A moist, brandy-soaked placebo by candlelight is just the thing for a solo Yule.

Drug companies put as much effort into the packaging and marketing of their products as go into the product itself. The colour, name, shape, dosage regimen and gift-wrapping are meticulously researched to maximise the placebo effect on top of whatever pharmacological action the drug may have. The vagaries of the human condition are such that anxiety responds best to green pills, depression to yellow and pain to red. A silly name adds to the aura, especially if it begins with Z, and the route of delivery is equally important. If you've just taken something large and oblong the French way, you'd be a fool to admit it didn't work. Likewise if you shell out nearly £7 on a prescription.

Fancy coloured pills also make it harder for the copycats. When a drug's patent runs out, me-too companies line up to churn out the stuff as cheaply as possible, which invariably results in small white tablets. Patients, however, are even more loyal to the appearance of their drugs than to their doctor. Hence it's virtually impossible to change them from the long yellow ones to the small white ones.

Bring Back the Placebo?

All treatments are part placebo, some more than others. If we evaluate them by the same standard, the randomised controlled trial, many – both conventional and alternative – have a job outperforming sugar pills and sham needles. But that doesn't mean they don't work. Placebos work very well.

We used to be able to prescribe Obecalp (placebo backwards) along with Pillula Panis (bread pills), Aq. Menth. Pip. (peppermint water) and The Pink Medicine (ingredients unknown). All were cheap, harmless and gave enormous benefit. But they're now considered unethical because they imply an element of deception (or at least not thinking too hard about the science).

But how can a pill with no active drug in it whatsoever work? The human mind is very susceptible to suggestion and expectation. The effects can be pleasing (hence *placebo* – 'I will please') or humiliating (a stage hypnotist turning you into a chicken on acid). The first documented use by a British doctor was in 1890 when a woman was given painkilling injections of water, believing them to be morphine. The jabs worked a treat but when she discovered the deception she called in the lawyers.

Placebos don't just make you feel better, they cause tissue changes. In 1986, patients with swollen cheeks after wisdom tooth extraction received ultrasound therapy to reduce the swelling. The jaws shrank by 35 per cent compared with a control group, not bad considering the probe wasn't even plugged in. They can also speed the healing of up to 70 per cent of duodenal ulcers. Go, that coloured blob of chalky love!

And they even work if you know you're taking one. If I say, 'I feel a so-called sugar pill will help you as it has helped many others. It has no medicine in it at all. Are you willing to try it?' it can still work but only if you believe in me. And I don't laugh. Placebo effects are increased by magic (healing energies, third eyes, meridians) and if it works for you, why not? We should never pooh-pooh the power of the Smartie. Especially the blue ones. Now who wants one of my Magical Healing Love Tablets?

Can Complementary Medicine Save the NHS?

Which brings me nicely on to complementary medicine. Who thinks it can save the NHS? . . . And who thinks it shouldn't be allowed in the NHS unless it's been proven to outperform a placebo? . . . About a fifty-fifty split, Druids and doctors.

Some doctors feel angry and even threatened by the popularity of complementary medicine. One consultant used to call the advocates of its use GROLIES – *Guardian* Readers of Limited Intelligence in Ethnic Skirts. That's quite an achievement. All medical bigotry in one acronym.

GPs are much more inclined towards complementary medicine than hospital doctors. That's because we recognise medicine is as much performance art as science, and there are lots of patients who aren't in the same play. Say you have pain, distress, despair, loneliness and tiredness that just won't fit into any of our diagnostic boxes. All the tests are negative. None of the drugs work. Something must be done. Consultants can discharge you from the clinic but GPs can't. If you get a benefit from complementary therapies, who are we to argue? They can meet your emotional and spiritual needs in a way that a blister-pack of ibuprofen just can't manage.

Edzard Ernst, Professor of Complementary Medicine at the Universities of Exeter and Plymouth, has devoted his career to examining the evidence and published the results in *Complementary and Alternative Medicine, an Evidence-Based Approach*. It includes the more mainstream therapies, many of which regulate and monitor themselves. But there's no urine therapy, radionics or butt candles. There isn't a clear case for including many of them in the NHS on the basis of evidence but the trouble with most trials is that they focus on hard clinical endpoints (death and disease), rather than quality of life, happiness and emotional satisfaction.

Controlled trials aren't usually representations of real life. Patients are carefully selected (or cleverly coerced), those who don't fit in are excluded, more trials are done on the young than the old, more on men than on women. So it's a tough ask to crowbar the best evidence based from, say, thousands of amorphous middle-aged men into the life of a frail eighty-eight-year-old woman who's already on ten tablets, half of which make her feel dizzy, and who lives for her cat.

Complementary medicine, on the other hand, starts with you (and possibly your cat), and tries to offer some interpretation while harnessing the body's capacity to sort itself out. Some of the jargon, theories and claims may be ludicrous but I can see why it's popular. Plus you get half an hour of you, not six minutes of me.

Rather like comedy, art and religion, whether you find something emotionally or spiritually uplifting is an individual thing. You can't always predict it on large clinical trials. I could never have colonic irrigation because it's very hard to put a hose up your arse if you're laughing. I've tried it several times on rugby tours. But I don't deny others the right to try it if they value the experience and perspective.

Placebos have a bad name thanks to a rubbishing from the drug industry, doubtless piqued by the amount of money they waste on trialling drugs that can't outdo chalk. But I think they're great. I regularly use masturbation, ice cream and dog wrestling to make me feel better (though not simultaneously). I'm not sure I'd sell them as therapies but they work for me.

Others prefer the power of positive thought backed up by fairy dust. There also seems to be a basic human need to believe in the unbelievable. The success of Harry Potter and the Old Testament isn't entirely due to the prose style. Medicine used to be magic, doctors used to be 'other', but we're endlessly demystified in the media. We're like magicians whose tricks have all been explained. So people are flocking to complementary therapies. 'I've got too much jitsu in my tsubo, you say? That'll do nicely – here's fifty quid.'

You can make up your own complementary therapy today and it'll work if you carry it off with enough conviction. But placebos only keep working if you keep the faith. And the best way of doing that is to serve them up with a big dollop of love. That's why they're so popular.

Eht Cigam fo Evol

Doctors aren't very good at love. If we're not emotional cripples when we leave medical school, it only takes a year or so in the NHS. Americans talk about having 'unconditional positive regard' for patients but you're more likely to get that from your dog than your doctor. We don't do love.

Complementary therapists, by contrast, are full of it. They listen to your pain, they acknowledge it, they individualise it, they interpret it. You're not just a number in a randomised controlled trial, you're a unique, overweight ginger GP desperate to be on the TV and with lots of emotional baggage. Let me carry it for you. Let me stick a pin in you. We will get better. Together.

The magical power of medicine has always been in the human effect. You need time and continuity with a lovely doctor, like Dr Rose, to really carry it off. Split medicine into little bits and you destroy its magic.

I've tried a whole range of magical loving, out of professional interest. Homeopaths believe that if you dilute something it gets stronger. The weaker the beer, the more pissed you get. They also treat like with like. Your remedy is based on a substance that, if given in large amounts to healthy people of your ilk, produces the same symptoms you are experiencing. A homeopath once gave me nux vomica (strychnine) for stress, because lots of strychnine makes fat, ginger doctors irritable, apparently. He was less interested in my homeopathic penis but at a push gave me extract of onion because a large penis makes your eyes water. And I met a man who'd been to the Royal London Homeopathic Hospital for an infinitesimally dilute solution of Berlin Wall to unite his disparate symptoms. He felt better and I haven't laughed so hard in years. So homeopathy helped us both.

A GP friend of mine learnt acupuncture in a weekend and tried it out on Monday. 'I'm just pricking your Encircling Glory, Mrs Fanshaw. Can you feel your Qi being renewed. No? Well, how about I stick it in your Abundant Splendour?' I had a go too but I had to stick the needles in my own hand to stop me giggling. I really do lack the emotional depth for this sort of thing.

I don't need magic but I do like touch. Anything at a distance leaves me cold. Radionics involves dowsing one of your hairs with a pendulum and plugging the results into an electronic box, which figures out your physical, emotional and spiritual well-being, as well as your risk of getting HIV, diabetes and cancer. Then by twiddling a few knobs, you reduce your risks.

How do you know it's working? I couldn't feel a thing but a lady called Imogen could. 'After two minutes, I was aware of a large circular globe of energy from about my navel to about my forehead, which gradually contracted down and focused very strongly on my throat. After a while, the energy slid up to my third eye and circled round in an anticlockwise direction. I've never experienced anything like that; very impressive.'

My favourite was inversion therapy, which had me dangling upside down, suspended on an acrobat's feet over Glastonbury Tor, while he chimed a Tibetan wedding bell. I'm still not sure if I felt better afterwards but he really cared for me. And technically we're married.

Touch Me, I'm a Doctor

Doctors are generally too busy medicalising you to love you. But I do know one GP who kisses his lady patients. We're not talking slobber on the knuckles or whiskers against the cheek – he hits them smack on the lips. When I did geriatrics, I was tempted into the odd peck (not just with the spinsters with large estates and no surviving relatives) and I assumed my colleague was doing likewise but no, he kisses women his own age. Once when they come in, once when they pull out.

I've checked with the GMC and I can apparently kiss you all, provided it isn't perceived as sexual. I think the ginger hair may help. If you'd like to form a queue.

I once worked with a GP who was a compulsive hugger of the elderly. His theory was that they can go for weeks without human contact and he was doing them a huge favour. Certainly he was terrifically popular, so much so that one mature lady started putting it about the supermarket that 'Dr Ron gives me cuddles.' This reached the local press and he was forced to move to Suffolk, which is a great pity because he was very good with the difficult patients.

It's easy for doctors to construct an argument to get them out of touching. True, there are some psychiatrically ill or confused patients whom it may be unwise to hug and some entirely rational patients who don't relish the arm-around comforts of a sweaty health professional but the vast majority of us find asexual human contact comforting in times of adversity. Indeed, massage therapists would argue that adversity is too late to discover the joys of 'unconditional stroking'.

How do I know all this? I once had a Watsu, or water shiatsu if you prefer. I was so desperate to be on TV, I took off my glasses, exposed my beer gut to the camera and was bent and pummelled in a boiling swimming pool by a strange bearded Dutchman. Pim de Griff is one of just three Watsu practitioners in the country. 'Most men have forgotten what it's like to be cradled by another man,' he whispered as he elevated the experience from physical to spiritual. The whiskers tickled a bit but the overall effect was surprisingly invigorating. And not in the least bit sexual. Honest.

There are plenty of patients I'd love to submerge in a hot tub: 'It's all right, Mrs Smallbone. The intimacy of aquatic bodywork represents a new way of being. Don't forget to breathe now.' Yes, the key to healing is human contact. If doctors want to keep up with the druids, we have to rediscover the power of touch. But first, we need to sort out people who want to be touched from those who don't.

This isn't always easy. If a man pitches up to Pim for a Watsu, he can be fairly sure he wants to be touched. But if the same man comes to me for a repeat of his gout medication, I'm not so sure. I have to get informed consent first. So I lean across and say, 'Would you like me to touch you?' or, to avoid confusion, 'Would you like me to touch you in that special way that only a doctor can?'

And I give them a questionnaire at the end. 'How satisfied were you with the way your doctor touched you today? Name three things you liked most. Name three suggested improvements.' I've tried this approach in my surgery for the last fortnight but it'll be a while before the results appear in *The*

Lancet. Preliminary findings can be found in the *Sunday Mercury.*

Can touching save the NHS? Every consultation should start and end with a big hug. And if you saw some of my patients, you'd realise how big that hug would be. Let's start now. Hold hands with the person next to you . . . That's good. Now go for the big full-on hug. Remember your doctor needs it as much as you do. We've all got baggage. Dead babies, tough targets and that cow of a night sister. Let it all out. And release . . . Excellent. Now doctors and patients can walk together hand in hand, as loving, equal, rational partners without the need for batty magic bollocks.

The Art of Bad Science

Some doctors get apoplectic about all the bad science out there. Ben Goldacre is both apoplectic and funny. His website (www.badscience.net), book (*Bad Science*) and – wait for it – 'Bad Science' column in *The Guardian* are required reading for rationalists. He even managed to get the same educational qualifications for his dead cat as 'Dr' Gillian McKeith. He's also young, handsome, brilliant in bed (results of double-blind trial pending) and not ginger. And he's talking to telly.

To prove I'm not bitter, I invited him on to the panel of my Radio 4 pilot, *Medicine Balls.* This book was supposed to accompany the series but Dr Ben ruined my chances by accidentally launching into a lengthy soliloquy about 'arse candling': 'If you go to the website buttcandle.com you'll find numerous lovingly hand-tooled illustrations of hollow candles gently drawing toxins out through the rectums of happy customers. The only reported danger is of the pressures created by the arse candle drawing haemorrhoids into the hollow channel of the candle, leading them to be tangled up in the hot wax.'

The BBC deemed this outburst 'inappropriate material for a

daytime comedy' and ditched the series. Bastard. But I've still ordered his book.

The TV, press and internet is chock-full of fat-dissolving soap and toxin-removing candles, and we used to laugh. But when middle-class mums got scared off MMR and started holding infectious disease parties for their children, some of whom are christened Rubella, it got beyond a joke.

The danger of suspending rational thought is that life requires it. Managing money, choosing treatments, ignoring health scares, understanding the universe and staying mentally healthy. It's hard to stamp out irrational, negative thoughts and feelings if you don't know what rational is.

I worry about people with terminal cancer spending their nest egg on radionics; I worry about people abandoning conventional cancer treatment for herbs; I worry about people camping in tropical swamp-land armed only with homeopathic antimalarials. But you can't force people to be rational.

In an entertainment age, science isn't popular outside China. No one knows how their PlayStation works, they just want to use it. No one knows why the light goes on, how old the earth is or what makes a plane take off. No one even climbs trees any more. Children are too busy having babies.

Science has its share of bias and corruption because it's practised by humans. But the idea – to observe, understand, interpret, predict and perhaps even cure – is pure. But to turn the tide against irrationalism and bad science, you also need to be human.

We are social animals. We need more than to be told we're wrong by someone with three degrees. We all need love, empathy, acknowledgement, hope and understanding. Less Henry Higgins and more George Clooney.

Does society have a paternalistic duty to protect people from being misinformed and ripped off? Some of the flakiest practitioners are far from being on the fringe. Buoyed by TV exposure and slick marketing, they dominate the health sections of bookshops. If we catch doctors or MPs telling mistruths, there's uproar. But we give flaky nutritionists calling themselves doctors free rein to peddle nonsense.

Bad science can only thrive through dodgy advertising and crap journalism. The key question in journalism is not 'what's the truth?' but 'what's the story?' Opinion sells better than fact. So if you haven't got a story, you just make one up. The beauty of health stories is that you can invent an unnamed researcher and quote unpublished research that no one can refute. It can't be challenged because no one else can read it.

Alternatively, selectively quote the few studies, or bits of studies, that support your argument while conveniently ignoring the larger number that don't. Then do a quick Google whack, cut and paste an out-of-context quote from an expert you've never spoken to, and presto! there's the story. You can print it safe in the knowledge that you're effectively unaccountable. If someone challenges you, it's about as rewarding as taking on the NHS. You have to be unbelievably persistent and anal to get a small retraction on page 13. The real battle for rationalists is with the media, not the butt candle.

Most of us need more than materialism and logic to get us through the night. Doctors can't provide the continuity and love they used to, so people get their healing effect and spiritualism elsewhere. Provided therapies don't make unsubstantiated claims about prolonging your life or curing you, then why not? Think of them as art, not science. They can take you to another place, give you another perspective and lift you up where you belong. Is that the Tibetan wedding bell calling me?

Can Art Save the NHS?
Art gives you escape, insight and emotional intelligence. Not easy to prove in a controlled trial but who thinks art is vital for

health? ... There you go. You can't fool all the artists all the time.

One definition of public health is 'the science and art of preventing disease, prolonging life and promoting, protecting and improving health through the organised efforts of society'. Not one man in a box writing prescriptions.

A major weakness of the NHS is that we focus on what makes you ill, rather than what keeps you well, and we're far more obsessed with the physical than the mental. Most people use art to stay mentally healthy. Stories are metaphors for life. They feed the brain and teach us about ourselves. We'd all be emotional wrecks without them.

So why not prescribe art on the NHS? There are loads of people who are a bit stressed and miserable but don't need antidepressants and don't want to see a counsellor. Literature, music and films lift the spirits and they can be consumed for the cost of a prescription, with fewer side-effects. How about trips to museums, galleries, concerts and the theatre? Writers and poets in NHS residence? Sensory rooms for anxious patients? Complementary therapy and chlamydia screening as performance art?

Consuming art is good for your mental health but making it is better. There are any number of creative therapies (art therapy, drama therapy, music therapy, pottery therapy, poetry therapy, therapy therapy), all helping us to communicate with ourselves and our environment. All are being gradually assessed by rationalists for proof of efficacy but usually the trials are too small or wrongly constructed to 'prove' anything.

As with teaching and doctoring, it's very hard to separate the power of the therapy from the charisma of the therapist. A music therapist who pumps up the volume beyond ninety decibels could deafen his clients. We need science to tell us that. But it's much harder to evaluate empathy, rapport, spiritual fulfilment and the intuitive ability to communicate.

I used to be a lecturer in medical communication. The rapport of some doctors is almost an art form but most of us need a bit of practice. The scientific approach to deciding how doctors should communicate is to split our discourse up into seventy individual, evidence-based communication skills that comprise something called the Cambridge–Calgary observation guide.

Each of these skills had apparently been proven to work in research where doctors and patients (or actors) change one skill at a time. I can't, with absolute certainty, name any of them. Fortunately I can guess most of them, because they could have been written by the Professor of Common Sense at the University of the Blindingly Obvious:

- Establishes appropriate eye contact
- Greets patient and obtains patient's name
- Introduces self and clarifies role
- Demonstrates interest and respect
- Identifies and confirms patient's problems . . .

Can I stop now?

You can't argue with them. As my mentor John Skelton pointed out, to argue the opposite would be laughable, so why articulate the obvious? This is how science doesn't work, when wrongly applied. It's ridiculous, it's boring and you turn off. As a student, I found it patronising in the extreme to be told I should greet a patient and establish eye contact. But I wanted to understand why doctors didn't always do it. Is it just the whisky? Or does he just not like people?

And when is eye contact appropriate or inappropriate? Who decides that? Do we need science to tell us how often we should blink or look down? Or do most of us do it instinctively for the culture we're raised in?

Some doctors communicate so poorly that they should

never have been let in. For most of us, the reason a consultation goes pear-shaped usually lies deeper than surface skills. We give patients who irritate us a worse deal. Not skill but attitude. That's what determines how we communicate, that's what science can't measure but art is very good at exploring.

So maybe art can save the NHS. But if we reduce it to tiny pieces and test it scientifically, I shan't read the results. The more interactive a therapy is, the more it relies on the brilliance of the therapist. You can teach and research performance skills and you can program them into a computer but it'll never win *The X Factor*. And if you're a sexist, homophobic bigot, it doesn't matter how you arrange the chairs. Unless there are public service values underpinning your communication, it's bullshit.

Art and Environment

There's always a furore when hospitals spend money on paintings or sculpture but we need a different perspective when we're ill. We need to know there's more to life than pathology, that we're more than just a bag of chemicals. Environment is vital to health. I couldn't spend more than a day a week sitting in a windowless box in the clap clinic.

War zone wards, dank waiting areas and grim consulting rooms make patients and staff ill. I once worked in a casualty department where the 'breaking bad news to relatives' room had no chairs. It couldn't have been designed to be more uncaring. Better than shouting death down the corridor but only just.

The concept of the sick building is nothing new. Large, poorly maintained and anonymous. Low ceilings, cramped offices, high room temperatures, lack of natural light and ventilation, damp, dirt, background noise and flickering fluorescent strip lamps. Many hospitals and surgeries tick every box. They seem to be designed to keep us all as sick as possible.

The idea of enhancing the patient environment was, until recently, seen as frivolous. But the environment defines the culture of an institution. I once interviewed patients about their first experiences of the NHS, and nearly all of them mentioned how unwelcoming the buildings were. It was as if the bricks and mortar were trying to turn patients away before they even got to the bearded receptionist.

The health service was built on rationing, and the last thing we wanted was beautifully designed hospitals and health centres that might encourage people to use them. Clap clinics were down in the basement as part of the punishment. The long walk of shame through the peeling tunnel to the (not so) special clinic 13.

The links between art and health have been recognised in all cultures, from the ancient Greeks onwards. In 1735, the artist William Hogarth painted a beautiful mural for a staircase at London's Bart's Hospital and Florence Nightingale observed both 'the suffering of a patient not being able to see out of the window' and 'the rapture of fever patients over a bunch of brightly coloured flowers'.

And they've even tried to prove it. In 1984, an American study compared two matching groups of patients recovering after surgery. One group had a view of a brick wall, the other looked out on to a rose garden. The latter needed fewer drugs and less pain relief, made better progress as documented in the nurses' notes and got out of hospital more quickly. As Prince Charles put it, 'It can't be easy to be healed in a soulless concrete box. The spirit needs healing as much as the body'.

Putting It All Together in Bromley-by-Bow
Health is complex – all sorts of things impinge on it. People have physical, emotional, educational and environmental problems and if you could come up with a way of sorting them all out, we might start narrowing the gap between rich and poor.

The most inspirational attempt I know of is the Bromley-by-Bow Healthy Living Centre in Tower Hamlets. It's been evolving since 1984 but the fact that it's flourishing in a climate of target-driven, tightly regulated evidence-based medicine is a miracle in itself.

The centre has a GP practice. It also has allotments, a gym, a community café, a computer training room, a garden, a cinema, a crèche, massage facilities, a pottery room, dozens of complementary therapies, a children's playground, employment training and after-school club facilities. It gets people into work, some of whom work on-site. With inspirational buildings and sculpture on three acres, it serves a very deprived population of 15,000 people, many of Bengali descent. The ethos is to nurture people in a setting that reflects the age range and ethnicity of their community. It's sure start, middle and end.

Patients aren't allowed to be passive. They're expected to personalise their health care and are invited to help the centre or their community; some produce artwork or help maintain its gardens. People are encouraged to rely less on doctors and more on their families and community. The staff sometimes shop and cook with their patients and support them in moving home or seeking a job.

Over 100 different activities are offered each week, and the centre works in partnership with other community organisations. The aim is regeneration by developing individuals and supporting community leaders.

There is good evidence that patients who are involved, and actively participate, in their health care do better. By defining health in its broadest terms and cementing participation into the culture, the Bromley-by-Bow project could achieve enormous benefits in a very deprived area. That's if it gets the financial and political support it deserves and the staff don't all burn out through overambition.

It's experimental, complex and changes too fast to make evaluation easy. But the approach has far more emotional intelligence and community insight than anything I've ever come across in the NHS. And it's hard to disagree with an ethos where people decide what makes them healthy. Some things you can't easily measure are immeasurably beneficial. We need to free the front line of the NHS, working with patients, to unleash all that pent-up creativity. Bollocks to quangos; let's have Bromleys in every city.

Can Darwin Save the NHS?

'It takes all the running you can do, just to keep in the same place,' said the Red Queen to Alice, an idea adopted by evolutionary biologists as the 'Red Queen principle'. If foxes start running faster, rabbits are naturally selected to run even faster, so that foxes must evolve to run faster still. If foxes' eyesight improves, this selects for rabbits that blend better with their background, which may select for foxes with a better sense of smell, which in turn selects for rabbits that learn to move downwind. Predator and prey always co-evolve in an increasing cycle of complexity.

I discovered this in *Why We Get Sick: The New Science of Darwinian Medicine* by Randolph Nesse and George Williams. It was recommended to me by Richard Dawkins, who believes that just about everything can be better understood in light of evolution. Even God. The Red Queen principle applies perfectly to bacterial resistance. Stronger and more powerful antibiotics ultimately only ever lead to stronger and more powerful bacteria, and the problems they cause, thanks to Darwin, are entirely predictable. So why hasn't the message sunk in?

In 1969, the Surgeon General of the United States was so chuffed with his antibiotic armoury that he announced 'it is time to close the book on infectious disease'. Alas, the writing was on the wall for antibiotics a quarter of a century earlier. In

1941, all staphylococcal bacteria were vulnerable to penicillin. But by 1944, some strains had evolved enzymes to break it down and resistance had taken a foothold. Today, nearly all staphylococcal strains are resistant to penicillin.

For each generation of doctors, the 'antibiotic fox' has got ever more powerful – in the 1950s methicillin came along and ruled for a while but, when I trained, methicillin-resistant *Staphylococcus aureus* was widespread and ciprofloxacin was hailed as the magic bullet that would never be beaten. Now nearly all strains of *Staph. aureus* are resistant. Give the 'bacterial rabbit' a chance mutation and a bit of time, and it always gets ahead of the game. Indeed, there is so much bacterial resistance around – tuberculosis, gonorrhoea, salmonella, *E. coli*, pneumococcus, clostridium – that some microbiologists believe we may soon have to face up to a 'post-antibiotic era', where Fleming's fungus and all its descendants are defunct. We need a new fox, and quick.

Despite repeated exhortations to use antibiotics with extreme care, we can't help prescribing them and you can't help asking for them. Add in the fact that animals are routinely dosed with antibiotics, as is much of the meat, milk and eggs we consume, and it's easy to see why bacteria have the upper hand. Punitive public health sanctions are politically unpopular and, in a consumerist society, it's far easier to give people what they think they want, rather than what they need.

We could reduce the spread of resistant bacteria by washing but that's something we also seem incapable of doing, especially men. In a small sample of my household, the females wash their hands before eating and after using the toilet, and the males don't. Likewise, many doctors don't wash their hands unless forced to. Maybe we still believe an antibiotic will sort out our dirty fallout. In the first twenty years or so of the NHS, cleanliness was next to godliness and Matron would decapitate anyone skimping on the soap.

Then Matron became extinct, we privatised the cleaning staff, everyone went in and out of the hospital in their increasingly dirty uniforms and dangled their bug-ridden ties all over the place. Wards became overcrowded, targets led to musical beds, isolation became near impossible and hand-washing twenty times an hour was never going to happen. So we threw antibiotics at it and the rest is history.

Not washing is such a deeply ingrained male trait that there must be some evolutionary advantage in it. Maybe, keeping a layer of grime mixed with your own bodily bacteria is a defence against colonisation with superbugs. Or maybe it makes it easier to catch rabbits. Darwin's greatest legacy is that everything has an evolutionary reason.

The Evolution of Patients

The more complex the organism, the slower the evolution. Which is why we'll never beat the bugs. The NHS is one of the most complex organisms on the planet, which is why it definitely can't beat the bugs. It evolves at the speed of a glacier. We've tried to change it, or at least disguise its inadequacies, by constant redisorganisation. But I think the only thing that'll work is a mass behavioural mutation of patients.

Are patients rabbits and doctors foxes? Or vice versa? Doctors kill patients sometimes, not always by mistake, but we generally don't eat you. And we'd prefer it if you got better and left us alone. Patients kill doctors slowly, by refusing to do anything we suggest, and occasionally swiftly with a bowie knife. But you'd prefer it if we got you better too, so you don't have to waste your brutally short lives hanging around the NHS.

Patients do better if they sort out their own health care instead of running to the doctor every time their nose drips. And all doctors are patients, very reluctantly, eventually. Ah yes, I see it now. We're all the same species. Either foxes or rabbits. You decide. But on the same team.

There are four, interchangeable groups of patients. Those who want complete control over their health and their decisions; those who want to be partners with people who ought to know what they're doing; those who want to be told what to do by people who ought to know what they're saying; and those for whom health is way down the list of priorities below money, sex, class A drugs, nappies and the avoidance of stabbing.

The British traditionally have an over-reliance on experts and an establishment that prides itself on telling us next to nothing. 'You do what you like, doctor, I'm entirely in your hands, you've got to learn somehow, etc., etc.' But the informed patient is slowly evolving extra fingers to access the internet and learn how to be awkward, rather than just good.

People who participate in health decisions do better, both psychologically and physically, but they also tend to be people who are in a position to participate, by dint of education and not being stabbed recently. Everyone deserves the chance to 'go Bromley' with their health care. And everyone should be offered access to the best information about health outcomes without having to ask for it thirty seconds before the anaesthetic kicks in.

If a critical mass of patients come out of the headlights and start asking for information, we'll have to give it to you and my guess is that publishing the best evidence (rather than star charts or Elvis adverts) will make the NHS, government and pharmaceutical industry up its game. But information has to be appropriate and paced. Drowning patients in a sea of risk factors because they've asked for informed consent is just childish. But often legally advised, to cover our backsides.

Better still, we could learn to stay healthy upstream without going anywhere near the NHS. The way to save the NHS is not to use it. Save the money for people who are really unlucky. But first I need a drink.

RICK

'Doctor, I've come to lobby you.'

'Have a seat.'

'I want colonic irrigation on the NHS.'

'This is one of Gloria's wind-ups, right?'

'Who's Gloria?'

'No one's asked you to invent some ludicrously improbable scenario?'

'No. I'm deadly serious. You bloody doctors are so dismissive of anything different, anything new, anything that challenges your "hack it out and plumb it into a Sainsbury's bag" view of bowel disorders. Well, that's too late for me. I'm not waiting until I get cancer. Flush out all the crud and toxins.'

'Have you finished?'

'Don't bloody smirk. I feel absolutely marvellous afterwards. It's the best feeling in the world.'

'Better than sex?'

'Different.'

'It's quite unusual for a man to have colonic irrigation, isn't it?'

'So?'

'How are you coping with life in general?'

'Don't give me that amateur psychology crap. I'm fine, work's fine, the family's fine and my colon's getting flushed out twice a year for the rest of my life.'

'Lovely. But I think the NHS has other priorities.'

'You don't even know what it involves, do you?'

'Not entirely.'

'See, you're writing something off without considering it.'

'OK, enlighten me. Who does it to you?'

'An East European in Clifton. She's batty as a fruitcake but she gives great lavage.'

'How big's the hose?'

'About ten pence in girth. There are actually two tubes. One to deliver the water, one to take it away.'

'What temperature?'

'Warm.'

'How much?'

'Thirty gallons.'

'Are you sure about that? There's a hosepipe ban.'

'Not all at once. It trickles in under gentle gravitational pressure.'

'And what trickles out?'

'Well, obviously there's shit to start with but every now and then you get this incredible warm sensation followed by a black cornflakey thing that's been stuck up there for years.'

'Splendid.'

'Better out than in.'

'And what position do you assume to have black cornflakes flushed out of your fundament with 240 pints of warm water?'

'You sit down, just like being in a dentist's chair. Only you can talk.'

'About what?'

'Life, the weather, the marrying of the cultures of Clifton and Eastern Europe. And there's Sky Sports.'

'Don't you worry that she might be flushing out helpful stuff, like bacteria?'

'Yes but she gives you bacteria tablets afterwards to replace it. And some herbal tonics. And you can have a coffee enema but that's extra.'

'And it's a great way to be kicked out of Starbucks. What does Lady Lavage think of your meat-heavy diet?'

'She thinks that's why I have so many black cornflakes of festering, putrid gristle.'

'Hang on a sec. How do you know what's coming out?'

'The tube that takes it all away is see-through.'

'Right.'

'And I feel great afterwards.'

'So you say. But I'm not sure that'll convince the PCT. These days you need a double-blind randomised controlled trial.'

'What does that mean?'

'Divide two groups at random, one gets irrigated and the other doesn't but nobody knows which is which.'

'You know when you've got a hose up your arse, believe me.'

'Maybe we should do a trial with two groups of volunteers having six-monthly hoses, but only one turned on, and see what happens to the rates of bowel cancer and irritable colon over ten years or so.'

'I can't wait that long.'

'Are you still smoking?'

'Yes.'

'That's a lot worse for you than having a few meaty cornflakes in your bowel. Does your washer woman do lung irrigation?'

'If she did I'd be first in the queue.'

'In the meantime, have some nicotine patches. In case of leakage.'

GARETH

'Thank you for coming back.'

'Thank you for working Wednesday.'

'How did you get on with my book?'

'OK. I'm not convinced you wrote it though.'

'Why?'

'Because you claim to be open to new ways of healing but you're still trying to force drugs on me.'

'You've got tuberculosis. Even Mrs Linton has her limits.'

'You told me TB was a purely physical thing. The bacteria are very hard for the body's immune system to digest and you need to take these poisonous drugs.'

'Powerful drugs.'

'Whatever. You need to swallow all these chemicals to get better.'

'True.'

'But it isn't. You're completely overlooking the importance that the mind can play in manipulating the body's immune response.'

'Is this Mrs Linton speaking?'

'No. Paul Martin. *The Sickening Mind*. You recommended it in your book.'

'How psychological and emotional factors influence health through their effects on behaviour and the immune system?'

'That's the one. What do you say, in a very patronising manner, to anyone who deigns to see you with a cold?'

'"The body has a remarkable capacity to heal itself"?'

'By George, he's got it.'

'But this is TB we're talking about here, not some poxy snot virus.'

'Once you get tuberculosis, whether it spreads or whether your body holds it in check depends a lot on your mental state. If you're depressed like I was holed up in that disgusting hospital, the TB gets the upper hand. But now I'm out and happy and surrounded by healing energy, I'm getting better without drugs.'

'Not for long you won't.'

'Sir Peter Medawar, the Nobel-Prize-winning immunologist, said TB is "an affliction in which a psychosomatic element is admitted even by those who contemptuously dismiss it in the context of any other ailment". As early as 1500 BC, Hindus observed that a main cause of TB was sadness. Hippocrates and Galen were on-message too. And before the twentieth century, when physicians actually took time to observe their patients meticulously, a cause of TB was said to be "a long and grievous passion of the mind". Then there's *spes phthisica*.'

'Wasn't he in *Emmerdale*?'

'The concept of the tuberculosis-prone personality. The artistic temperament. Why do you think all those nineteenth-century luvvies gave in to consumption if it wasn't for an excess of aesthetic emotion?'

'Because they all crammed into the same garret, shagged like rabbits and coughed all over each other.'

'So you don't believe your mind has any effect at all over your body?'

'Of course. Embarrassment makes you pink. Lust makes you purple. Fear can trigger a heart attack. People die just after their partners. Depression increases your risk of a heart attack. But remember 1882.'

'Why?'

'Robert Koch discovered the real cause of TB. *Mycobacterium tuberculosis*.'

'Yeah. And all you bloody scientists suddenly forgot about

the importance of emotional factors in illness and became obsessed with bacteria in your haste to discover antibiotics and earn billions for the evil pharmaceutical giants.'

'I think you're being a little unfair. The drug industry has been responsible for some great advances in medicine.'

'Well, you *would* say that, wouldn't you? You're all in their pocket.'

'They pay for all my education. And some of the reps have fabulous breasts. But that doesn't affect my clinical judgement. I just want you to get better and not infect those who aren't lucky enough to have your third eye.'

'We all have a third eye'

'Is it brown?'

'It could be.'

'I think I've found mine.'

'What would you have done in the days before drugs?'

'Packed you away to get lots of fresh air and sunshine.'

'And did anyone get better?'

'Yes. But lots died. Between the seventeenth and nineteenth centuries, TB was one of the biggest killers of all. It's still one of the major causes of death in Third World countries and disturbing pockets are appearing in the UK amongst the homeless and those who are HIV-positive.'

'Yeah but I've got a home, I'm HIV-negative, I eat well and I'm seeing a healer. So I could survive without drugs.'

'True. But you could infect more vulnerable people on the way.'

'I'll just try not to cough on anyone.'

'I've got a better idea. What if you take the drugs to kill the bugs and use Mrs Linton and her healing energy to protect you from side-effects?'

'Will it work?'

'I don't see why not. If she can heal George Bush, she can stop your piss going red.'

'I'm not sure.'

'It'd be like an amazing fusion of the best of conventional and complementary therapy. Truly integrated medicine.'

'Can I think about it?'

'No. Give it a bash for a week and let me know how you're doing next Thursday.'

'Wednesday.'

89 MINUTES TO SAVE THE NHS
Part Three: How (Not) to Be a Patient

Can patients save the NHS? Labour has this phrase for the health reforms: it's called Shifting the Balance of Power; STBOP. In the Department of Health, it's known as Shifting the Blame onto Patients.

The state of the NHS is partly our fault. For years we've slagged off politicians for lacking the moral courage to campaign for increased NHS funding but we wouldn't have voted for them if they had. We're all in the dock for this; it's our collective responsibility.

Not that you'd suss this from your average casualty department on a Saturday night. It's like a battle scene from *Lord of the Rings*. People celebrating the joy of human existence by drinking nineteen pints of snakebite, headbutting the receptionist and stabbing a nurse. In my local casualty department, they wear slash-proof gloves to fend off the machete attacks. As an obstetrician once confided to me, 'The worst part of my job is helping the British to reproduce.'

Keeping Mum
And what are you going to do with Mother? Long-term care of the elderly fell off the NHS under the Tories, and no one wants to look after their relatives either. Some people treat their kin worse than their pets. You wouldn't dump your labrador in casualty or stick her in a distant nursing home for years on end, come down once a year and yell at the vet, 'Something must be done.'

People are far more upset when their dog rolls over than

when Granny dies. Because dogs give you unconditional love and they die with happy memories and dignity. Whereas Granny is forced to struggle on in a foul mood with no memory, fouling the bed and with an empty shell for a brain.

The NHS no longer does cradle to grave, we do cradle to until your brain goes to putty. The least we could do is care for the carers. Failing that, let's all move to Scotland.

Labour wants to put patients at the centre of the NHS, which is of course the middle drawer of the mortuary. But I think *you* can save the NHS. By not using it.

Not Using It

Maybe the problem is not that we don't have enough doctors or nurses but too many patients. The NHS is an open invitation to medicalise our lives. If you make a service free at the front door, then anyone can phone up with any problem at any hour of the day. Lavatory won't flush? Call NHS Direct. Wasps' nest under the eaves? Summon your GP. Fancy a curry and haven't got the taxi fare? Dial 999. Feeling a bit miserable and lonely? Go get some happy pills.

A friend of mine was called urgently to see a patient marching down the street, balancing a glass eye on the end of his proud penis. No hands. It's a great trick, worthy of an audience, but it doesn't have to be a doctor. A photo would have done.

A free service means people sit in casualty with paper cuts or go to the GP every time their nose drips. If you closely analyse the million or so GP consultations and hospital attendances that go on every day, the percentage where you can prove the patient has derived any benefit from being there is surprisingly small. The cost of mumbled reassurance is huge.

I lead by example – I last visited a GP's surgery twenty-six years ago. I was naive and nineteen, with very big tonsils and I thought I had glandular fever. So I went to student health, this bloke put his hands down my pants, had a good feel around and asked me what I was studying. I said 'medicine' – he took his hands out pretty sharpish and mumbled something about inguinal nodes. Haven't been back since.

I didn't find out until years later what it was all about. Why do doctors grab on to your testicles – if you're a bloke, obviously – and ask you to cough? And the answer is: because it's a laugh. A bit of fun. Halfway through a morning surgery, feeling a bit bored, just grab somebody's bollocks. Makes the day go quicker.

But the main reason I don't go down to the doctor's is I feel fine most of the time. And when I don't, I watch a movie, have a tug and get some kip. Works for me. I haven't got a clue what my cholesterol, blood sugar, PSA or body mass index are. Dr Rose insists on taking my blood pressure once every few years. But she is lovely.

I might come a cropper with a silent killer but I'm reasonably well off, I try to keep my belly in check and live with the risk. And I take one of Dr Phil's Magical Healing Love Tablets every day.

The Secrets of Health

Let's suppose you're lucky enough to live where shit happens several times in a life, rather than three times a day. You've got a few bad habits but having sex with your children isn't one of them. You want as much money as possible to go on building Bromleys for poor people, so they won't joyride outside your house and steal your chattels. And you want to enjoy your life, whilst avoiding the NHS and thus saving it in the process.

What is Health?

One small problem with staying healthy is that no one can agree what health is. The word is everywhere – health service, health economy, Department of Health, public health, healthy living, health and safety, Norwich Community Health Partnership – but there has to be more to life than just not being ill.

The World Health Organisation reckons health is 'a state of complete physical, mental and social well-being'. That's as good a definition of an orgasm as you'll find. But what do you do for the rest of the year?

According to the Royal College of General Practitioners, health is 'a process of adaptation to changing environments, to healing when damaged and to the peaceful expectation of death'. Whoop-dee-do. Where's the fun? Where's the adventure? Where's the excitement? Clearly not in the Royal College of General Practitioners. Risk is important for health; the trick is to control it. Nude wrestling in wet cement is generally safe. Driving down the wrong side of the M6 with a head full of crack is less so.

Men will always seek adventure and take risks with our health. We'll always average lower life spans than women. We don't want to end up the only bloke at an Age Concern luncheon club (although in these post-Viagra days . . .). And we'll never abandon a weekend of shin-kicking and beer-swilling for a warm community centre, a slice of lentil bake and a group discussion on better foreskin hygiene (wash behind with water only, give it plenty of air and let it dry before you peel it forward). I expect to die before Dr Rose. But not from cancer of the penis.

Expectation and Failure

Another definition of health is the extent of the gap between expectation and achievement. If you achieve what you want, or what's expected of you, your life is less of a bitch than if you're constantly striving to hit some impossible parental expectation, literacy level or bureaucratic target. The NHS is a profoundly unhealthy place to work in because it always promises more than it can deliver. Each successive government cranks up the expectation and, with it, the sense of failure and misery even if it's doing OK.

If you're branded a failure when you're young, it could spur you on to great things but it's more likely to steer you to crime, drugs and deprivation. And poverty will always be the biggest predictor of ill health. People need work and something they can occasionally succeed in. Other than pregnancy.

Why are we less happy now than we were in the fifties, despite living longer and owning more? Probably because living longer and owning more don't make you happy. Living in a great community and having time to enjoy and enhance it does. The trick with aspirations is to have the right ones. We can't all be Joseph but we can all smother his brothers in body butter. Or something like that.

Staying Sane

'You've got to ac-cent-tchu-ate the positive, e-lim-inate the negative . . .' If we all took his advice, the world would be much healthier, happier, creative, positive and successful. So why don't we? This seems to be the question behind *Staying Sane*, Dr Raj Persaud's self-help thesis on preventing mental illness. At 654 pages, it's a touch too passionately argued for me but I think I've got to the nub of the argument. We live in a very negative culture and this negativity trickles down into our lives. Most of what parents say to children, and spouses say to each other, is negative.

According to Dr Raj, all this negativity breeds Automatic Negative Thoughts or ANTs, which are the roots of our unhappiness, anxiety and depression. So what's the solution? Page 358. Here we are: 'To stop my daily RANTS against myself, I must kill my ANTs.' Personally, I prefer 'ac-cent-tchu-ate the positive, e-lim-inate the negative', written by Johnny Mercer for Bing Crosby and the Andrews Sisters in 1944. So who prefers

Johnny's pre-Hiroshima homily? And who likes Raj's ANT rant?

Johnny wins hands down. Which is amazing, when you think about it. How could a humble songwriter with no mental health expertise develop such a sophisticated theory of staying sane over fifty years in advance of Dr Raj Persaud, Consultant Psychiatrist at the Bethlem Royal and Maudsley Hospitals and Gresham Professor for Public Understanding of Psychiatry?

Much as I love Raj, I'm not convinced that severe mental illness can be prevented. There are some patients who just can't stamp on their ANTs. Because they're fifty feet tall. And telling you to kill all the infidels. But most of us are social animals and need the emotional ballast of love, friendship and community to thrive.

You also need to thrive on your own. Mentally healthy people tend to be self-reliant and enjoy disappearing inside their heads. Success is more likely if you're an optimist but some people just aren't no matter how many self-help books they read. Raj does however have some useful advice on parenting. Be very careful what you name your children. People with uncomplimentary initials (e.g. P.I.G. or D.I.E. or B.U.M.) apparently have worse mental health and die three years younger than average, whereas those with positive initials (A.C.E. or V.I.P. or F.A.B.) feel better and live three years longer than average.

Lots of books are about 'the power of belief', as if belief in itself is a good thing (in fairies, doctors, Gods, healing energies, love tablets). The teachings of John Lennon are particularly confusing here. First he invites us to imagine a world without religion and possessions. Then he tells us that whatever gets you through (or rather thru) the night is all right.

As a doctor I find it generally doesn't help the therapeutic relationship to challenge someone's cherished beliefs, though occasionally I have a Dawkinesque moment. When I'm inside my head, I believe in the evolutionary ability of humans to sort themselves out without reliance on astral beings or medical paternalism. But in my six minutes with a patient, I often slip into TV doc dogma because I'm lazy and I want to be home in time to play with the children.

Some psychologists believe behaviour is far more important than belief. The trick, apparently, is to own your emotions. If you hit someone, it's your fault not theirs. Even if they did call you a ginger, speccy twat. And hit you first. Officer.

Anger Management and Artificial Saliva

Oh what it is to be human. No other species habitually destroy their own for fun but we seem to have evolved an unquenchable thirst for cruelty, ruthlessness and revenge. Lots of us really enjoy aggression. As one of my friends put it, 'People keep blathering on about how awful road rage is. Well, I need it. It's an essential part of my life. It gets out all of my frustration at the end of the day. If I don't get the chance to wind down the window and yell "For fuck's sake, you dozy cow!" on the way home, I take it out on the wife. It ruins the whole evening. But if I've had a good rant, I'm as sweet as pie. I've banged on a few roofs but I've never hit anyone or forced a car off the road. So what's the problem?'

Bob sees road rage as some sort of necessary catharsis, possibly for the frustration of lack of sex and achievement, although we haven't discussed it that deeply. But on the few occasions I've driven with him, I've wished I hadn't. Ironically, Bob cured me of the delusion that the expression of aggression was a good thing. For as long as I can remember, I've been prone to bouts of violent temper. I blame the red hair; my brother thinks it was because our father died when we were kids. Whatever the cause, I swallowed Freud's view that aggression, like flatus, was better out than in. Allow it to dam up, and mental illness results. So I took up rugby.

Being ludicrously short-sighted, I had no fear and waded in recklessly. I had my nose broken several times but I usually felt better for it. The college team consisted of fourteen swotty myopics who had to be pointed in the right direction, and Bob. We won a surprising number of matches given the haze we were playing in, and started an unsurprising number of fights, given that we couldn't see where we were treading.

In the second year, I was made captain and wore contact lenses, so I could greet the opposing captain and rally the troops. I took it very seriously but Bob took the piss. I tried to lead an amateur haka, a deeply spiritual and skeletally impossible warm-up exercise that involved stamping your feet and punching the air simultaneously. Bob stood outside the circle, fag in hand, and laughed. What hope has a team got when it can't even show respect for its own haka?

From that day, the bubble burst. Bob convinced me that I looked like a twat when I tried to get angry, and I convinced myself that playing in contact lenses was a lot more scary because you could spot the hard bastard on the other side. So I stopped playing rugby.

I thought I'd miss the weekly violence but I didn't. I took up satire and read up on anger. There's no evidence that expending your aggression on a sport's field or in a car makes you any less aggressive when you've finished. On the contrary, aggression just seems to breed more aggression. Those who indulge in contact sports exhibit far more daily aggression in season than out of it. The reason they find it cathartic is not because legally controlled violence makes you mellow afterwards – it doesn't – but simply that they enjoy being aggressive.

As for me, I've found a brilliant solution to road rage. It's called artificial saliva, available over the counter for people without much real saliva. It's great for public speaking, when one end of your gut goes dry and the other end goes moist. Squirt it on your tongue it actually tastes like someone's spat in your mouth. But best of all, I keep it in the glove compartment for when someone cuts me up. Instead of stabbing them, I calmly lower my window and fire off a few squirts, without a hint of anger. Virtual gobbing. You know it makes sense.

Real Men

Is it good for men to express emotions other than aggression? Many women (and therapists) spend their lives encouraging men to share their emotions (after owning them, of course). One study compared the 'emotional expressiveness' of men who'd had heart attacks to those of similar age who hadn't. The results found that men who found it easy to express their emotions were fifteen times less likely have heart disease than the bottlers.

This is a small trial and possibly meaningless. It might be that the experience of a heart attack had made the men less likely to express their emotions for fear of rekindling bad memories or putting strain on the heart. And just because 99 per cent of vicars wear pants, it doesn't mean pants make you believe in God. Do vicars even believe in God? Does God wear pants? Science is complicated. Far easier to hug.

The proposed link between personality and heart disease is not new. In his excellent book, *The Sickening Mind*, Paul Martin charts the history of the 'coronary prone personality'. For centuries, doctors and healers have proposed that hostility, impatience and naked ambition can take their toll on the heart. In 1910, the physician Sir William Osler wrote: 'It is not the delicate neurotic person who is prone to angina but the robust, the vigorous of mind and body, the keen and ambitious man, the indicator of whose engine is always at full speed ahead.'

In 1930, high blood pressure was put down to 'repressed hostility and anger' and in the 1950s, two American cardiologists called Friedman and Rosenman set about proving their observation that ambitious, competitive, impatient men were most at risk. Their research found that 28 per cent of these 'Type A' men had heart disease compared to 4 per cent of relaxed 'Type Bs'. These men did express some emotions but they tended to be hostility and aggression. So not all emotions are better out than in.

One study of over a thousand Type A men took a random selection and gave them counselling aimed at reducing their hostility and sense of urgency. It halved their risk of a heart attack. And in 1997, a study by the British Heart Foundation found that meek, gentle women who prefer to give in to others are less likely to have a heart attack than assertive women. Roll over, Germaine.

So, how can a personality type lead to a heart attack? The mechanism is probably down to how we react to the everyday stresses in life. American research found that fiery-tempered people are three times more likely to suffer heart attacks than those who don't rise to the bait, and the likely culprit is the stress hormone cortisol. Heart attacks occur when the arteries to the heart firstly narrow with fatty plaques, and then a plaque ruptures and blocks off an artery completely. High levels of cortisol make this rupture more likely. Cortisol also eats away at a part of the brain called the hippocampus and makes us prone to depression. And recent research from Denmark and Canada has found that depressed patients are far more likely to suffer heart attacks.

Does depression cause a heart attack or is it the other way round? There is evidence that 'Type A' people are prone to burnout but the heart risk is likely to start a lot earlier. If you're always psyched up and on the go, your pulse and blood pressure tend to be higher and even if you enjoy the stress of your job, your heart won't necessarily enjoy the high adrenaline and cortisol levels.

But the main effect of personality on heart disease may come down to behaviour. Type A people are more likely to eat trashy food on the go, to smoke and drink heavily and to find giving up harder. They seek out conflict and are more likely to live alone, with little social support. There is strong evidence that marriage is great for a man's heart, but even then he may not talk to his partner much. Type A men ignore symptoms, are less likely to admit they're ill and simply don't have time to go to the doctor. And being in denial about chest pain is very bad news. So tell her how you're feeling but don't get angry about it.

Work, Stability and Control

A nurse I know was given a depression questionnaire to screen her patients. Keen to understand what she was going to put them through, she tried it out on herself. Bad idea. The unexamined life may not be worth living but scrutiny has its side-effects. 'Are you basically satisfied with your life? Are you in good spirits most of the time? Do you think it is wonderful to be alive now?' By the end of the shift, she'd discovered that the staff were more depressed than the patients.

Each year, work-related stress costs UK employers £500 million, and society at least £5 billion. Half a million people a year report work stress at a level that makes them ill, and many more are too frightened or ashamed to speak out. The figures are increasing but the causes aren't clear. Is work getting harder or are we just becoming a nation of wimps? Years ago, we sent small boys up chimneys and they never complained. We were much less healthy and died en masse in our fifties but no one dared turn up with a sick-note citing 'occupational stress'. Today, work stress is less about losing a limb in the canning factory and more about failed expectations.

So who's in control? A study of Whitehall civil servants found a clear gradient in health at every level of the hierarchy. Once you've matched them for age, sex, weight, exercise and bad habits, the one factor that seems to keep people alive is control itself. Which is why politicians are so keen to keep hold of it.

Lack of control and entrapment are at the heart of our best sitcoms: Basil Fawlty trapped between Sybil and Manuel, Blackadder stuck between Queenie and Baldrick, Alan Partridge and David Brent stuck in soul-destroying jobs. Ring any bells?

Without work, all life may be rotten but it's not great with too much either. Workaholism is the hidden addiction, just as lethal as any other -ism, but expected in American and British culture. If you ditch the materialism, money gets less important and you can take your foot off. People generally worry about money and sex before health. If you don't mortgage yourself up to the apricots, you'll enjoy the sex more and find yourself strangely healthy. And when the going gets tough, remember the three Ps: pace yourself, pamper yourself and piss yourself laughing.

Mental Health and Love

Mentally healthy people tend to be positive, even when shit happens. My theory on why comedians get depressed is that most humour, particularly satire, accentuates the negative. If you obsess about finding a negative slant on life, it comes back to bite you. When I first did *Have I Got News For You*, I made the near fatal error of reading every newspaper for a week. I've never been more depressed.

My father suffered from depression and committed suicide when I was seven. But I've so far been able to beat the black dog. Escaping into story-land helps. I find literature a much better way to understand humanity than counselling. A friend of mine who lost his wife after fifty years was offered antidepressants by his GP: 'I said I'd rather not medicalise my condition and was coping adequately thanks to the medication provided by Dr Chekhov. I still wonder if he thinks an East European immigrant has joined a rival practice.'

Loving, caring and being part of a community are things that science has been poor at evaluating and yet they probably contribute far more to our health and sense of well-being than any number of drugs.

The effects of love deprivation were discovered in post-war Germany. Children growing up in two orphanages, close to each other and with identical food rations, were studied. In the Bienenhaus orphanage, the children suffered under the tyranny of the stern and forbidding Fräulein Schwarz. They put on less weight and grew less quickly than the children in the nearby Vogelnest orphanage, cared for by the affectionate and warm-hearted Fräulein Grun. Then, part-way through the study, the grim Fräulein Schwarz took over at the Vogelnest orphanage. Despite having more food now, the children did not thrive and their rate of growth declined.

Physical Pleasures

I am either unbelievably healthy, or in denial. Here's how I do it.

Diet, Body Hair and Alcohol

We're all stuck in a rut. The trick is to make your rut as comfortable as possible. Let's start with diet. The Japanese eat less fat than us and have fewer heart attacks, the French eat more fat than us and have fewer heart attacks. The Japanese drink less red wine than us and have fewer heart attacks, the French drink more red wine than us and have fewer heart attacks. Eat and drink what you like. It's speaking English that kills you.

I take loads of fruit and veg, usually orally, fish when I remember, and I try to buy local for fear of being drummed out of Britain's greenest village. But I eat and enjoy just about anything, usually far too quickly. Especially nuts. Instant gratification.

I've met people with all sorts of complicated lists about what food they think makes them ill. But they never have a corresponding list of food that makes them well. Why not? Start with nuts. Unless you're allergic. Or morbidly obese.

I don't diet or weigh myself – a sure route to misery – but if the tops of my legs start rubbing together, I walk and cycle more. And I remove all my body hair twice a year. Back, crack and sack. It reduces the ginger-ness and makes your knob look double the size. Just like in the movies.

The trick with alcohol is to treat it like a medicine, a modest amount most days except when you might have to steer or brake suddenly. We've known for years that moderate drinkers live longer, on average, than both teetotallers and heavy drinkers. Alcohol reduces your risk of heart disease and since this is our biggest killer, and gets more common as we get older, there is an overwhelming case for moderate drinking from mid-life onwards. Officer.

Sex

Another great study found that men who have a hundred orgasms a year reduce their risk of death by 30 per cent. Now I'm not a mathematician but I've worked it out: a tug a day, you're immortal. Got to be worth a try:

'What are you doing in there?'

'Just staying healthy.'

Generally men and women have better orgasms if they do it themselves, so there's really no excuse. Proper sex is good for men too, at least twice a week. Professor George Davey Smith and his Bristol colleagues studied 1,222 men aged forty-five to fifty-nine in Caerphilly and five of the villages around it. The men were assessed according to blood pressure, cholesterol, etc. but also their frequency of sex. Two hundred and twenty-nine men fell into the 'high' category (i.e. twice a week or more), 490 men were 'medium' (i.e. less than twice a week but more than once a month), and 190 were 'low' (i.e. less than once a month). The men who had the most sex were non-manual workers with slightly higher cholesterol levels than the once-a-monthers.

Over the following ten years 150 of the men died, sixty-seven from heart disease and eighty-three from other causes. But the more sex a man said he had per week, the less likely he was to die. The high sex group had half the risk of dying than the low sex group. Don't use this for emotional blackmail. You may not get the answer you want.

Whether it's sex or just orgasm that's good for men is unclear. All the men in the study were married, which we know is good for a man's health too, and it seems that some men claimed to have sex twice a week despite being married for ten years. However, the study didn't specify who they had sex with.

For women, it's quality rather than quantity. One study in 1976 found that sexual dissatisfaction was a risk factor for women having heart attacks, with premature ejaculation and impotence in men being major underlying factors. Other studies have shown that women most value foreplay, foreplay and more foreplay. If you're too lazy for that, Liquid Silk and Replens are much better lady lubes than KY Jelly.

But maybe we need to lower expectations here. The calorie counts for different acts have now been worked out. Putting a condom on an erect penis uses up just three calories. Trying to put one on a flaccid penis burns off 12,674. A real orgasm uses up only ninety-six calories but a fake one is 62,856. All that huffing, puffing and pretending can be a really good aerobic workout. So even bad sex can be good for you. That's my excuse, anyway.

Walking
An orgasm is the equivalent of going for a leisurely stroll but do we need more exercise than that? Yes, but it doesn't have to be torture.

All you have to do is walk up a hill, once a day, until you get a bit puffed and sweaty. You don't have to join a gym and torture yourself in public. If you've forgotten how to walk, your GP can now prescribe exercise therapy. My senior partner has discovered an amazing cure for apathy – bungee jumping. They don't come back.

Walking is unbelievably good for you. One study looked at its effect on the longevity of 16,000 Finnish twins, aged 25–64. The twins were divided into couch potatoes (no real physical activity), occasional exercisers (get out for a decent walk less than six times a month) and conditioning exercisers (people who did some vigorous walking or a spot of jogging for thirty minutes at least six times a month). They were followed up for seventeen years during which time their exercise patterns really didn't change much. Quite a few of them died over this period, mainly from heart disease or cancer. But the difference that regular, simple walking made was enormous. It reduced the chance of death over the seventeen-year study period by 60 per cent.

Another large study done in Honolulu came up with very similar results. Men who walked two miles a day had about half the chance of dropping dead over the ten-year period studied than the couch potatoes. There is no form of medical intervention or pill that gets close to having such a big impact on our health as walking.

Dogs
Walking is even more fun with a dog. If we could prescribe dogs on the NHS, it could save it overnight. A dog gives you unconditional love, communicates with your autistic son, reduces your cholesterol and blood pressure, improves your mood, gets you out walking and talking to other dog lovers, and it keeps you supple as you pick up the crap. And if you're too depressed to put your pants on in the morning, he'll lick your balls. You just don't get that with Prozac.

Airy Naps

After a brisk dog walk, I'm partial to a nap. Without enough sleep, you're more prone to infections and perhaps even cancer. You can torture prisoners to death just by sleep deprivation. The damage kicks in after just one night of poor sleep but is far more of a problem in the long term. The metabolic and hormone changes of chronic sleep loss mimic those of ageing, and increase the risk of diabetes, high blood pressure, obesity and memory loss. You can't cheat on your sleep. The good news is that it doesn't matter when you get your kip. Lie-ins, catnaps and siestas are all excellent ideas, unless you're driving or at war.

I sleep with the window open. Modern housing tends to be hermetically sealed and although every man likes the smell of his own farts, there has to be a limit if you want your lungs and relationship to thrive.

Pleasure

It's also important to pleasure yourself every day, not just in a gentleman's way. Enjoyment is an entirely personal thing but the concept spans every culture in every time zone. And there are some common denominators. Alcohol has been invented and used in every culture known, even (or especially) when it's banned. Sex, stories, chocolate, pets, music, dancing, laughter, caffeine, sunshine, driving too fast and perfume are just as ubiquitous. There is a basic human need for risk and enjoyment. Control it but don't deny it.

Why don't we study pleasure? If you scan the medical research databases, nearly all the mentions of it are in the negative sense (e.g. the absence of pleasure as a feature of depression), and in the *Oxford Textbook of Medicine* pleasure gets just two mentions (in relation to condom usage and physiotherapy), whereas stress weighs in with 127. As with our news media, medicine is obsessed with accentuating the negative rather than the positive. Why people get sick rather than what makes them healthy. Maybe that's why doctors are so depressed.

Passion
Passion is as important as pleasure. Often you can combine the two. Gardening and *The Archers*. Sex and *Countdown*. Evolution and labradors. Antiques and chutney.

Give Blood
Blood donors live longer, either because it thins the blood or because the type of people who become donors are more sorted. Or maybe they get their anaemia picked up earlier.

Laughter
Laughter is very good for you. People who laugh a lot seem to get fewer coughs and colds and they may even get less heart disease and cancer. But instead of being left alone to decide what you think is funny, there are now dozens of laughter therapists popping up, teaching us how to laugh.

I was so offended by this medicalisation of laughter that I signed up for a course, just for doctors. It was called 'Ho Ho Holistic Health Care'. We weren't allowed to laugh at the things doctors traditionally laugh at, such as other people's misfortune, but instead we had to lie in a circle, join hands and 'release the joy of the inner child'.

Then we were invited to have fun. A bald man came on with his juggling balls. Two women did something unusual with a piece of cheese. By this time, I was starting to doubt the healing power of laughter until Jay, our group leader, took me to one side. 'Dr Phil,' he said, 'I want you to forget all the routine advice you give to your patients, day in day out. Exercise, diet, smoking, lifestyle – forget it. It's boring, it confuses people, it doesn't work. And drugs are passé. I want you to start prescribing fun.'

A week later I was back in the surgery, sitting opposite Malcolm, who suffers from recurrent whooshing in his toes and an itchy nose. I was about to tell him to go away and phone NHS Direct when I remembered Jay's wise words. 'Malcolm,' I said, 'when did you last release the joy of your inner child?' He wasn't so sure about that, so I changed tack. 'When did you last have fun?'

'1963.'

'It's time you had some more. I'm prescribing fun, three times a day; avoid milky drinks.'

Off he went and had some fun and all his irritating symptoms disappeared. Until he was arrested for showing his knob to a lollipop lady. One man's fun is another man's gross indecency. You can't be too prescriptive.

As you get older, you tend to rate contentment and regular motions above belly laughs, and you're happy just to get through the night without getting up to pee seventeen times (although there are pills for that now. See your GP).

Dropping the Kids Off at the Pool

Passing a big, fat, solid-yet-soft motion is one of the great pleasures known to man. But it's not just about being well hydrated and full of fibre. You need the toilet seat to be low enough to allow a natural unfurling of the rectum. As we get older, we tend to raise the toilet seat so we can get off it again but it makes for a much less satisfying drop. It's your choice.

How to Be a Patient

Pill Popping

How many people here are on multivitamins? . . . About half. We're already getting more than we need sprayed all over our cereals. Who's on hormone replacement therapy? . . . Just you, sir? And a lovely moist pate you have too.

Women generally take it for three months or so, get bored with it or scared off it. Apart from my mum. She loves HRT, she always demands the latest, so her GP's given her the new testosterone patches. They're fantastic. Made her even more assertive, way out front in the pension queue. She's got just one side-effect, though: she's got a little bit of unwanted hair. On her penis. Still, that's medicine for you – swings and roundabouts.

I don't swallow a thing apart from my own Love Tablet but I'm amazed what you can buy over the counter. Nurse Syke's Powders, Red Kooga Beetalife, Hoffel's One-a-Day Garlic Pearls. What is this stuff? As Lily Tomlin put it, reality is just a crutch for people who can't cope with drugs.

The big growth area is depression. It's going to catch us all – health scares, terror attacks, family breakdown, debt, workaholism, unemployment, fluctuating hormone levels – so try to put some money in Prozac shares before you get too depressed. When I qualified, people got antidepressants if they were depressed and we managed to spot it. Now they get them if they're just a bit pissed off.

In America, children as young as three get antidepressants. A mate sent me this cutting from the *Brooklyn Courier*: 'Alistair Gorrie, an expatriate living in Brooklyn, was recently diagnosed as clinically depressed, tanked up on anti-depressants and scheduled for controversial Shock Therapy when doctors realised he wasn't depressed at all. Only Scottish.'

September 11th was a huge boost to the antidepressant industry. In October, an advert appeared in the *New Yorker* magazine saying 'Millions of Americans are feeling anxious, millions of Americans could be helped by Paxil.'

Dr bin Laden, don't tell me you're just another drug company flunkey? Remember – antidepressants aren't addictive. Until you try coming off them.

I'm not saying drugs don't work; they're just overpriced and oversold. There's a rather dull discipline called evidence-based medicine where worthy people abandon their families and search all the trials about a given treatment. They discard about 80 per cent of trials as rubbish – no controls, biased, fraudulent, whatever – and they search out the good ones, especially the unpublished ones hidden under the stairs that show a drug doesn't work. Then they try to lump them all together.

The interesting thing is that if you're taking tablets every day to reduce the risk of something nasty happening to you in the future, it always comes down to a sentence like this: 'If a hundred people like you take this tablet every day for five years, one life will be saved but I don't know if it'll be yours.' And we wonder why people don't swallow.

But we keep trying to force them. As medicine becomes politicised, patients get medicalised. Instead of just getting you well enough to do the things that made you sick in the first place, we're expected to lecture you on your bad habits and chase down your risk factors. Come in with a bunion, go out with a statin. 'So sorry to hear your dog's died. We'd better just check your blood pressure.' Doctors should respond to the patients, not coerce them into treatment.

Last week, I was going through a pile of repeat prescriptions, and loads of people were on ten tablets a day, some of which I'd never heard of. The only way I know if they're safe to take all together is if the computer tells me. There was an eighty-five-year-old woman on twenty-eight tablets a day. Two for blood pressure, two for heart failure, two for cholesterol, three for diabetes, two for brittle bones, three for arthritis, two for indigestion, two for constipation, three for pain and seven for the obsessive compulsive disorder she'd developed since taking all her tablets.

She was also on warfarin, to reduce the risk of stroke but her blood levels were going up and down like a bride's nightie, even though she swore she was taking the tablets. So I called her up. Turns out she got so confused about which tablet to take when, she just emptied a month's supply of all her drugs into a shopping bag and took twenty-eight out at random each day: 'I figured it would all even itself out in the end.'

One bloke called me up to complain that I'd changed his tablets because 'the first lot sank when I flushed them and these ones float'. Go round to people's houses, open the cupboard under the sink and there's a sea of statins and blood pressure pills, in between the Fairy Liquid and the pilchards.

Unless a drug does something you want, makes you see pretty colours or gives you an erection, you're unlikely to take it for long. It costs billions to develop drugs and pay doctors to prescribe them, yet we swallow less than half of what we're told to. Always have done, always will.

The establishment solution to this phenomenal waste of money has been to bribe GPs to prescribe more, rather than less. If we play join-the-dots medicine and hit all our targets, we get enough money to send our children to private school, and your mum gets enough drugs to fill an extension to the cupboard under the sink.

Most drugs chip away at the risk of something unpleasant happening, like a stroke or a heart attack or a fracture. But the more drugs you throw into the mix, the more side-effects you get. Some people can stomach loads of tablets, some can't and some just don't want to. We should celebrate diversity, not force patients to comply. If someone wants a cholesterol check, fair enough, but I hate tricking them into it when what they popped in to talk about is their sick pig.

It's like going to the superstore to buy a bedside table and they insist on selling you a bath and a wardrobe with it. If you decide you don't want a new bath, you should be left alone. But if you decide you don't want a cervical smear or a blood pressure check, you'll get a series of reminders in the post before you're 'exception reported' and branded a 'non-complier'. Whatever happened to patient choice?

Here's the deal. If you don't want to be medicalised and you aren't going to take the tablets anyway, don't come and see us. We'll only make you anxious. We'll give you a label like high blood pressure, you'll think your head might explode and you'll stop the things you enjoy, like sex and joyriding.

Compliance

If you're on a ludicrous number of tablets, take them to your pharmacist and ask her to divide them into three piles: ones you really ought to take, ones which you could take for maybe half a year and ones that can be stockpiled for a Soviet invasion. Then take the essential pile, pop them in an envelope and send them to Glaxo, with a note asking if they could be made into one single tablet. True, it'd be the size of a Wagon Wheel but, if we smothered it in marshmallow with a caramelised chocolate coating, I'd be first in the queue.

And why not combine recreational drugs with conventional ones? What are you more likely to take, a blood pressure tablet that makes you fall over when you stand up suddenly or a blood pressure tablet that makes you stand up suddenly, dance and hug people? And then fall over.

Figure out the tablets you really need to take and politely decline anything that makes you feel worse than before. Don't cash in the prescription and then just stockpile the drugs. Wasted pills cost the NHS a fortune. If you're not going to take the treatment, what benefit do you get from going to the doctor? Reassurance and love are hard to find in six and a half minutes. Especially if you don't do as you're told.

Prevention

There are different types of prevention. The type I like best is where you keep mind and body in trim so you don't need to go anywhere near the NHS. The other type is when doctors or nurses do something to you to try to cut down your risk of something nasty happening in the future. It can save your life but it can also have side-effects.

I'm glad I'm not a woman. Not just because of the periods, birth pain and cracked nipples. But you just can't escape medicalisation. According to American screening junkies, a woman should have, between the ages of forty and sixty-five, thirteen BP checks, five cholesterol checks, six smears, fourteen breast examinations, fourteen checks of breast self-examination techniques, eleven mammograms, thirteen stool occult bloods, three tetanus immunisations, six smoking history checks, six alcohol checks, six family function enquiries, one session of menopause counselling and one session of pre-retirement counselling. And a partridge in a pear tree. That's if she's perfectly healthy. And she has health insurance.

A friend of mine who runs a cervical screening programme doesn't have screening herself. It would cut her risk of an already rare cancer but it might also cause her worry, inconvenience and unnecessary treatment because of common, slightly abnormal results. She's weighed up her personal risk – non-smoker, few sexual partners – and decided it's low. If you're prepared to take the hit for the risk you should be allowed to do so, not persecuted.

A mate of mine who describes himself as a fat bastard who drinks and smokes too much paid £200 for a private health screen. He came back pleased as punch.

'How'd you get on?'

'They say I'm a fat bastard who drinks and smokes too much.'

'I'd have told you that for a fiver.'

Americans take screening terribly seriously. A new website not only exhorts men to examine their testicles but also to do their own rectal examinations to check for bowel cancer. What you're looking for is something that feels like a button mushroom stuck to the side of the rectum. Of course, it could conceivably be a button mushroom. We tell you to take five portions of fruit and vegetables a day but we don't tell you how to take them.

The Rolls Royce of unnecessary screening is the whole-body MRI scan, being rolled out in private clinics across the UK. We have fantastic scanning technology but we don't have the research to understand what it means. Look at anyone's body closely enough and you'll find the odd spot or shadow somewhere. You assume the worst and worry like shit until you fork out another £3,000 for a repeat scan six months down the line, when they discover your first lot of spots have cleared up but you've got a few somewhere else. And so your life repeats as a VOMIT – Victim of Medical Imaging Technology.

Screening isn't compulsory; it's your choice. It's whether you want to medicalise your risk and reduce it with early intervention. Or live with it. Screening should keep you upstream but it doesn't always.

Birth

Should we march with or against the tide of medical progress? Women of sixty can now have babies. Is that a good thing? I suppose you don't have to push. It just falls out at the end. And you could breastfeed standing up. Or from the next room. Just let them abseil down. Older parents are much more fun. Who needs Alton Towers when you've got a stairlift?

Childbirth is a great example of medicalisation gone mad. Loads of people my age were born at home. These days, it's just 1 per cent. And half of them unintentionally, in the taxi on the way in.

In 1994, a large UK study found home birth to be safe for mothers with normal pregnancies, with half the risk of having either an assisted vaginal delivery (forceps or vacuum) or Caesarean section. Provided the midwife is competent enough to recognise the rare occasions when transfer is needed and it happens swiftly, home births for low-risk women, around 30 per cent of pregnancies, are safer than hospital.

But you do need enough experienced midwives and rapid access to hospital in an emergency. Which we don't have, so 99 per cent of babies are born in delightful, beautifully lit, sparkling clean maternity units.

And if you're really lucky, you may get the option of the birthing pool. How normal is that? Squatting naked with Vivaldi wafting through the speakers and the extended family – three existing children, the au pair and a couple of damp retrievers – splashing about in the foam. 'Come on, Jocasta, push into tomorrow, push into next week, push into the New Year!'

All encouragement is welcome but you only shout 'Push through your bottom' once. Out popped the most enormous turd I'd ever seen. A double-hander. I couldn't fit it in the sieve. The mother said, 'Is it a boy or a girl?' and the father said, 'How much does he weigh?'

'I'll just pop him on the scales for you, sir. Ooh look, he's got your hair. Well, one of them. Thought of a name yet?'

Shit Happens

OK, what if you have to use the NHS? You wake up one day and you've got a lump somewhere or you can't move something or feel anything or there's a nasty stain on the sheets. Shit happens to us all eventually. So what should you do?

Don't Die of Embarrassment

Embarrassment kills. I once met a man who let his testicle swell to fifteen centimetres – larger than a grapefruit – because he was embarrassed at having a lump down below and, as it got bigger, he was worried that the doctor would think he was an idiot for leaving it so long. It wasn't until it really pressed on the nerve endings that he sought help. He survived his cancer but lost a testicle that might well have been saved if he'd come earlier.

My default mode is both sceptical and optimistic but I'd rush my testicle down to the doctor if I found a lump. Bleeding or discharge from any orifice and lumps on or in any appendage should never be denied, however embarrassing. Put the book down now and make an appointment.

You Are What You Wear
Tip number one is to do what your granny said and dress up to see the doctor. Research published in the *BMJ* found that we try harder to resuscitate you after a cardiac arrest the more educated you are. As most people who've suffered a cardiac arrest have some difficulty with the questions 'Did you go to a good school?' and 'What was the date of the battle of Naseby?' I assume we judge you on appearance.

So next time you get crushing chest pain, phone 999, chew an aspirin and ask your manservant to go to the wardrobe for your cardiac arrest suit. Black pinstripe with a bright blue tie is best. Goes with the lips. Suits work well on women too, although a nice frock and a squirt of Rive Gauche will suffice. If you want to make absolutely sure you bypass the trolley queue in casualty, pin 'Friend of the Professor' to your lapel. And plenty of foundation for that ten-years-younger look.

A friend's child fell off the washing machine. She was wearing her grubby gardening clothes when she took him up to casualty and she got the third degree about non-accidental injury. A week later, the same thing happened. The staff should have been more suspicious second time around but she breezed in and out. This time, she had her smart clothes on.

The NHS tends to give a better deal to middle-class patients: longer consultations, more health education and even quicker referrals, although perversely this doesn't seem to increase their satisfaction with the service. Middle-class patients not only complain more but do it more effectively and get a second opinion to discover their baby really does have a dislocated hip. Those without nice clothes tend to get less return for their frustration, become desensitised and give up. In one study, a video of deliberately bad doctor–patient communication was shown to a group of inner-city mums, nearly all of whom judged it to be OK. The NHS survives because those whose expectations are low balance out those whose are high. But it shouldn't be that way.

Manner

NHS staff also tend to give a better standard of care to people they enjoy treating. Unfair because the 'moody buggers' generally need it more. A friend of mine was on a neurology ward with two women who'd both suffered similar left-sided strokes. One had lots of friends and relatives, remained outwardly cheerful and the nurses lavished lots of attention on her. The other had no visitors and was miserable as sin. She was also far less likely to recover without more help but she got far less attention. No one diagnosed her depression.

I was once asked to write a Good Patient Guide. I refused because I objected to the word 'good'. It implies doing what's expected of you and shutting up. I've seen elderly women wet the bed in hospital because they don't like to cause a fuss and ask for help. Assertive patients generally do better, more so if it's couched in humour rather than aggression.

Bribery

A builder once told me how he managed to secure excellent care for his elderly mother. He was going to send her to a private hospital for her operation but worried that they didn't have the expertise if something went wrong. So she went on the NHS but he 'bunged a few of the nurses fifty quid in cash'.

'They didn't accept, surely?'

'They were pleased as punch. And my mum had a ball. They were like bees round a honey pot.'

'Didn't you worry that it might deprive other more needy patients of nursing care?'

'Yes but when it's your mum . . .'

Rules of Engagement
Doctors tend to crystallise a single style of communication fairly early on in their career and stick to it. The eighty-year-old gets the same patronisation as the eight-year-old. I once recorded my consultations and was horrified how many times I said 'Listen to your body' and 'The body has a remarkable capacity to heal itself'. But at least I didn't say 'Your body is like Humpty-Dumpty. Once you've broken it, it's very hard to put you back together again.' Promise.

As a patient, you've got to decide whether you want to maximise the placebo of blind trust – 'I'm entirely in your hands, doctor' – or ask a few difficult questions. The balance of power in medicine is still very much in favour of what doctors would like to do to you, rather than what you might need when you're ill. Nobody gives unbiased information, not even doctors. But it's an effort standing up for yourself when you feel like death, which is why so many people end up entirely in our hands.

If you want to play the game, remember that any consultation can end up anywhere. There are so many things we could talk about – life, symptoms, the weather, whether the photos on the desk really are my children – that before you know it your six minutes are up and you've forgotten why you came here.

Try at least to get your reasons for coming (preferably in order of priority and fewer than six) out early on in the consultation, rather than at the exit. If your symptoms fit into, or can be forced into, a common diagnostic box, that'll be the diagnosis you leave with, whether it's right or wrong. If they don't, it'll be a virus, stress, life or, occasionally, 'I don't know but the body has a remarkable capacity to heal itself . . . If only you would listen to it. Humpty.'

GPs work on the basis of common things are common, so the rarer your disease, the more likely you are to end up with a wrong diagnosis, at least for the first few visits. I used to teach communication skills to doctors using actors who were amazed at how they could take the same set of symptoms to the different doctors and get completely different diagnoses.

So I tried it myself. I'm no actor but I can role-play a depressed alcoholic GP with great conviction. One doctor told me to pull myself together; another gave me sleeping tablets. One was very worried he might have to cover my patients if I went off sick. Of the four who diagnosed my depression, one gave me Prozac, one suggested St John's wort, one wanted me admitted to a private psychiatric hospital and one wanted me to enter a trial of cognitive behavioural therapy by computer. None picked up that I was drinking a bottle of vodka a day. I guess that's just normal for GPs.

In the discussion afterwards, it transpired that four of the GPs had suffered depression themselves but none had sought help because of the stigma and professional ramifications. Three had self-prescribed, one with an antidepressant that went out with the Ark. If you ever get the impression your GP isn't really listening to you, that could be why. Those persistent enough to get a second opinion are often amazed how different it is.

If you get a referral to hospital, it's vital to get the right department, even if it's the wrong diagnosis. If you get in the right bit of a hospital, NHS treatment can be second to none. If you get referred the wrong bit, it can be a disaster because doctors are now so specialised, they only diagnose within their box. The good old days of the generalist who could spot anything from primary biliary cirrhosis to secondary syphilis are gone.

The commonest reason for ending up in the wrong box is anxiety on the part of both doctor and patient. A lot of the referrals to neurology clinics to rule out brain tumours, chest pain clinics to rule out angina and gut clinics to rule out cancer are long shots but, in these days of defensive medicine, doctors are taking on less responsibility than we used to. But if your main problem is anxiety, rather than a brain tumour, the last thing you need is to be strapped into an MRI scanner.

Another common reason for ending up in the wrong box is that we don't listen to you, or don't register what you're saying, so we miss the symptoms that might lead elsewhere. This is more likely to happen if you have something less common. You get fobbed off with a virus for the first three visits, then we do some tests, then we say, 'There's something not quite right here. I think we'd better refer you but I'm not sure where.' A year after you first came to see us.

If you get referred to the wrong department, then the whole process can repeat itself ad infinitum until the oldest doctor in the hospital, who gets wheeled out for rare syndromes and special occasions, realises you've got secondary syphilis – or probably tertiary by the time they picked it up.

On the way, you'll have been placed in lots of other diagnostic boxes that didn't fit but if you try to crawl out of them or tell the doctor the pills are making you worse, rather than better, you'll probably be branded 'difficult'. Doctors don't like to be wrong. But we'd be wrong a lot less often if we listened more to patients.

I once saw a man who liked a drink and kept falling over. For the first few visits to different GPs, it was put down to the drink. His symptoms got worse and by the time he saw me, it was clearly more than the drink, although he still smelt very heavily of alcohol. I did a neurological examination and I thought he probably had Parkinson's disease. Turned out he had a brain tumour. But at least I sent him to a department where the right diagnosis could be made, rather than Alcoholics Anonymous on a Tuesday evening. Which he went to after his surgery and is now fit, well and off alcohol.

In some circumstances, like chest pain and meningitis, you don't have time to fanny around getting the diagnosis wrong, which is why you're encouraged to make your own diagnosis and get into hospital quickly, usually bypassing the GP. In Scandinavia, a lot of people over fifty carry an aspirin around with them, because if you take one while you're having a heart attack it dramatically improves your survival rate. In the UK, most people can't even do basic life support. And they sit at home with really bad chest pain, chewing Rennies until they turn Chelsea blue.

Chest Pain

Chest pain lasting fifteen minutes or more is a heart attack until proven otherwise. Don't fanny around. Phone 999. Chew an aspirin. Dress up. Try to look famous.

Other Emergencies

Sudden loss of anything – sight, movement, feeling, breath, blood, condom, consciousness, the will to live – requires urgent medical assistance. This does not apply to your cat or wallet.

My Meningitis

Doctors are no better as patients. I've only ever once been ill, with meningitis. Thankfully it was viral, otherwise I'd be dead.

As an adult, I pride myself on staying reasonably healthy and not wasting the NHS's time. Plus I hate the thought of being a patient. And then having to make one of those sickly confessions about how awful it was, and how I resolve to be a much nicer doctor in future. So here it is.

We were living in Birmingham, we'd just had our second child and Dr Rose was ever so slightly sleep-deprived. I'd been vomiting like that nice woman in *The Exorcist* for three days ('You should try having morning sickness') and as for the headache, I've never known pain like it, doctor. My head didn't actually turn through 360 degrees but it felt like it. When it persisted long enough for me to miss two episodes of *EastEnders*, the GP was summoned, against my will. Gavin was excellent – friendly, kind, thorough – but I could tell from his expression that I was headed for hospital.

'This vomiting – it's always in the mornings and relieves the headaches?'

'Yes.'

'That's slightly[1] worrying.'

'Yes.'

'What do you think we should do?'

'You tell me – you're the well doctor.'

'You're going to hospital.'

'Can I drive?'

'No.'

'Is it serious?'

'You should be fine. I've already had my brain tumour.'

This sort of cryptic reassurance is what doctors give to sick doctors. Brain tumours are mercifully rare, and each GP is likely to see one, or rather a patient with one, in his or her professional lifetime. Gavin had already seen his, so it would be statistically unlikely for me to join the club. Unfortunately two of my friends, both younger than me, had recently been found to have brain tumours (one benign, one not so lucky) so the old 'one in a lifetime' line was less of a comfort than it might have been.

---

[1] Note over-reliance on the word 'slightly'.

So to hospital, to see a consultant neurologist. 'I can't find anything much on examination but we ought to do a CT scan and a lumbar puncture.' That's what I love about neurologists. None of this 'What are your concerns? You must be very worried. Would you like me to hug you?' Just crisp, courteous, clinical detachment. The CT scanner was a bit noisy and it pinched my love handles but it showed a larger than average brain without any tumour but packed full of fresh and amusing insights into medicine. (Note: This is a joke. CT scans are very clever but they can't spot insights. You need an MRI scan for those.)

As for the lumbar puncture, well, I wasn't looking forward to a needle in the spine. Imagine my joy when up popped a junior doctor I'd taught communication skills to.

'What are you like with pain?' asked George.

Not one of my best students. I felt sorry for George – fancy having to stick a needle in your teacher – but he was up to the task. First he had to get teacher to strip down to his boxer shorts and curl up in the fetal position. Then he had to anaesthetise him.

'I'm going to use a yellow needle,' said George.

'Great.' (Yellow equals small.)

'I'm colour-blind though, so I have to be careful.'

George gives a great anaesthetic, which was just as well as it took him three goes to do the lumbar puncture.

'I'm in slightly[1] the wrong place here.' (Pause.) 'Where did you train?'

'Cambridge and St Thomas's.'

'Have you done many lumbar punctures yourself?'

'Yes but not on myself.'

'Nurse, could I have another needle?'

At last George was in and my spinal fluid was dripping out into bottles. Two hours later, the results were back and so was the consultant.

'You've got a hundred white cells in your CSF. I should say you've had a viral meningitis.'

'Will the children get it?'

'No.'

'Will I get ME?'

Cryptic smile.

'Can I go now?'

'Yes but don't be a typical doctor and drink large amounts of alcohol.'

'I thought I had to lie flat for six hours after a lumbar puncture.'

'We used to think that but there's no proof it does any good. Off you go.'

As I started packing, Sister approached.

'What are you doing?'

'Going home.'

'You can't. You've got to lie flat for six hours.'

'But the consultant said it was pointless.'

'Never mind him. It's the protocol.'

At 7 p.m., George reappeared and I explained my dilemma. 'Lie still for half an hour until the nurses change shifts and I'll smuggle you out of the fire exit.'

As I left at 7.30 p.m., full of praise for the NHS, the medical team were still on the wards putting in hours they would never be paid for. As George bundled me out the back exit, I asked him what job he was doing next.

'Haematology – so it shouldn't be too bad.' Leukaemia, lymphoma, myeloma – not too bad? Get me out of this madness.

Your Meningitis

Viral meningitis doesn't kill, or I'd be dead. Bacterial meningitis/septicaemia does. Fortunately it's rare but that also makes it hard to diagnose. I've seen the spots appear in front of my eyes and it's the scariest thing imaginable. You may not get any spots at all but you need to trust your instincts and get help, especially for children who just aren't right and can't be comforted. Symptoms can appear in any order and some may not appear at all. Here are some pointers . . .

- A fever with spots or a rash that do not fade under the pressure of a glass tumbler is a medical emergency. Phone 999.
- Early symptoms of meningitis can include fever, headache, feeling sick, being sick, muscle pain and fever with cold hands and feet.
- Babies and toddlers may get pale blotchy skin, food refusal, a dislike of being handled, an unusual cry or moaning, rapid breathing, grunting, floppiness, listlessness, drowsiness, unresponsiveness.
- Children and adults may also complain of a stiff neck, headache, stomach cramps, diarrhoea, dislike of bright lights, irritability, muscle pain and confusion.
- If someone is ill or is obviously getting worse, don't wait for spots or a rash to appear. They may appear late or may not appear at all.

Medical Language
The main reason you come a cropper when trying to take on doctors is that we talk bollocks. In my first few years at medical school, I learnt more new words than a student of Russian. Plain English was anathema and absurd labels were handed out like candy. We spoke of menorrhagia, rather than heavy periods, and dysmenorrhoea, not painful periods. And let's not forget oligomenorrhoea (infrequent periods), amenorrhoea (absent periods) and – wait for it – polymenometrorrhagia (frequent, heavy, irregular periods). Travel an inch or so upwards and you can have dysuria (painful wee), haematuria

(bloody wee), anuria (no wee) and polyuria (lots of wee). And let's not forget my favourite: borborygmi (tummy rumbles).

Jargon allows doctors to communicate quickly but it's also used to preserve the power, status and secrecy of medicine. If you can't understand us, how can you challenge us? Of course we wouldn't get away with it without your complicity. Also, there are a fair few people out there who enjoy being sick and for them a fancy diagnosis is essential. 'You've got a sore shoulder' is no use at all but 'You've got a supracapsular bursitis' gets you out of sex, work and the washing-up for at least a fortnight.

Doctors also have a proud history of euphemism for avoiding anything emotionally demanding. I once worked for a consultant who'd describe serious illness in cricketing analogies. Patients were either 'batting on a bit of a sticky wicket' or it was 'time for a short walk back to the pavilion'. The very notion that we might tell you the truth is surprisingly recent. As recently as 1993, a study found that 60 per cent of European gut specialists still wouldn't routinely tell a patient if he or she had cancer.

GPs are generally more colloquial, because we don't understand the big words either. Next time you visit, count how many times your doctor uses the word 'pop'. 'Pop on to the couch, pop your little panties down, I'm just going to pop a finger in, pop a sample into reception and pop back and see me in a week's time if you're no better.'

GPs are also renowned for hedging, the subtle evocation of the uncertainties in medicine. Listen carefully, and just about every consultation comes down to 'I'm not entirely sure what the diagnosis is but I'm fairly certain it's nothing too serious.' Or, if you prefer, 'It's probably a virus.' If the symptoms don't go away, you might get a few blood tests coupled with 'a possibility it might be something slightly more serious'. If you're really unlucky, you might be offered 'weeks rather than months' but nothing is definite. As George Bernard Shaw put it, 'A medical degree is no substitute for clairvoyance.'

Choices or Decisions

Choice is everywhere in health but I associate it with breakfast cereal or jam. We all have a right to choose; if there are too many choices we just go into meltdown but who cares, it's only jam. Don't sweat the jam stuff.

Decisions are more consequential. Deciding whether or not to have your leg amputated may be something you want to do, or something you want a doctor to guide you with. Generally, people seem to do better psychologically and physically if they're involved in the decision making, even if they leave the final decision to the experts.

OK, let's work through an example. Say you've had chest pain, your GP refers you to hospital and, after various tests, a surgeon tells you that your best option is heart surgery.

How many people here would just go with the flow and do what the doctor suggests? That's fine to trust people. No one knocks on the door of a cockpit and asks how many times the pilot has landed the plane successfully. Mind you, the fact that he's still alive gives us a bit of a clue.

So about a third would accept the recommendation of the expert and keep his placebo as big as possible. Who would ask questions? . . . Lots of you. What would you ask?

'Have you got the right notes?'

Good one. You'd be amazed how commonly we mix up notes and X-rays, even in these days of computers. I recently prescribed norethisterone to a bloke to stop his heavy periods on holiday. And if the World's Greatest TV Doctor is making such elementary errors, imagine what's going on in the rest of the NHS.

Out of interest, how many people here have read their medical records? You've been allowed to since 1992. And the answer is . . . Just you, sir. Why?

'I thought they had my diagnosis wrong.'

And did they?

'Yes.'

You're not a plant, are you?

'Well, I was according to the original diagnosis.'

Reading your notes is fascinating, although you probably won't understand them and they'll charge you for it. But once you cut through the acronym crap, you often disagree with the diagnosis and the priority of the problems. And sometimes they won't be your notes at all. So you can contact the person whose notes you've been given, sue the NHS for breach of confidentiality, split the money and retire to Barbados.

The idea when Labour came in was for us all to have electronic records which patients could own and carry round on a computer stick and even correct if they want to. But it's the NHS and it's computers, so it won't happen in our lifetime.

Before 1992, doctors used to use disgraceful abbreviations like FLK – Funny Looking Kid – usually with one or more FLPs. But we tend not to use them now as they're not so funny when read out in court. The same goes for resuscitation. In the old days, ten medical students would dive on your chest, crack your ribs and nick the chocolates. Then, when you'd died, they'd all line up to practise putting a central line in. But now relatives are invited to watch, they're far more sedate affairs and we try to disguise the smell of burning skin with Shake 'n 'Vac.

OK, any other questions you might ask someone offering you heart surgery?

'Why?'

Very good. Could you elaborate?

'Is it really necessary? What are the alternatives? How likely is it to improve my life expectancy and quality of life compared to, say, staying on medication or having an angioplasty? What if we did nothing?'

Excellent. Are you a doctor?

'I'm an economist.'

The theory is that we'll do far less heart surgery in future because everyone's on statins and blood pressure tablets, and we can blow up arteries with balloons and put tubes called stents in to improve the blood supply to your heart without hacking a great hole in your chest. Sounds great but all the research into and training for stents is sponsored by the people who make them. Some results look promising but can you trust them? When technology moves so quickly, often you end up with toys for the boys without hard evidence to back them up. So my guess is that we'll do just as much heart surgery as before, only on older patients after their stents have blocked off.

OK, any other questions?

'How long will I have to wait?'

Very British.

'What's the best treatment money can buy?'

Very American.

'Will it be painful? Who'll look after my cat? Who'll pick up my pension?'

Yes, all right.

'Will I get to meet the surgeon and the anaesthetist beforehand? What are the staffing levels like on the post-op ward? Do they have enough free and staffed intensive care beds? What's the level of MRSA?'

So many good ones. You can shut up now. How about if you decide to opt for surgery? What specific questions might you ask?

'Have you done this before?'

Always a good one. And if he or she has?

'Have you done enough of these to have meaningful outcome data?'

And if he has?

'What are your results?'

Not bad. Could you frame it in a slightly more challenging way?

'Will I die?'

Very good. Could you make it even more personal?

'How likely is it that you're going to kill me?'

Bingo. That's a great question, that very few people have the balls to ask. Who here would look down the barrel and ask a surgeon how likely he or she was to kill you? Maybe start with maiming. Or maybe accentuate the positive. How likely is it that you will improve my quality of life? But we don't usually collect that data.

Most people don't ask the questions and worry that if they did, they might get confused by the statistics as the anaesthetic kicks in. In an ideal world, all this information would be provided for you so you don't have to ask for it. You can't give informed consent without knowing the odds of coming through the other end but you want to make sure you're getting the correct odds, rather than some number plucked out of the air.

Informed Consent

Other doctors got to the other extreme and force too much information and jargon on patients in the hope of beating you into submission and covering their backs if shit happens. A Kent GP sent me a copy of a letter from a neurosurgeon at his nearest teaching hospital:

> I reviewed this 68-year-old lady in outpatients today. She has been having low back pain and right leg sciatica for about two years ... I have offered her an L4/L5 discectomy. I have told her that the risks include, but are not limited to, complications of anaesthesia, bleeding, infection, development of neurological deficit for example weakness and numbness of legs, problems with bladder or bowels, CSF leak, no improvement in current signs and symptoms, worsening of present signs and symptoms, death and other seen and unforeseen complications. She understands and wishes to proceed.

According to the GMC, 'doctors must respect the right of patients to be fully involved in decisions about their care, and the risks and benefits of individual procedures.' Fair enough but you need to judge the moment. When a relative of mine had a heart attack, he was offered not only a clot-busting injection but a comprehensive list of potential side-effects (nausea, vomiting, bleeding, back pain, reperfusion arrhythmia, intracerebral haemorrhage, rash, flushing, uveitis and Guillain-Barré syndrome). With the list came an estimated probability of each adverse event. After the pain and anxiety of a heart attack, and the sedation of a heroin injection, he was ever so slightly confused.

I see lots of men enquiring about a PSA test for prostate cancer. Most doctors think PSA stands for 'promoting stress and anxiety' because it's neither sensitive nor specific enough to be a useful screening test. But it's the only one we've got for a disease that kills 10,000 men a year. Because the test isn't very good, and the proof that having treatment for prostate cancer improves the length or quality of your life is far from perfect, I give men a detailed discussion and an information leaflet (they can choose between a one-page, three-page or five-page version) to enable them to understand the implications of testing. I then send them away for a week to think about it. But after all this effort and reflection, every patient asks, 'What would you recommend, doctor?'

The government now wants to give you a choice of five different 'providers' every time you're referred for hospital treatment. But for it to have any meaning, you need to have the answers to a few basic questions about each unit. How likely am I to die or be severely damaged by having or not having each treatment? How likely is my quality of life to be improved by having, or not having, each treatment?

If you're a statistician, and the pain isn't too bad, you could then bamboozle the doctors by discussing their figures in terms of funnel plots, regression analysis and confidence limits. The NHS needs to publish the best information, adjusted so as not to prejudice doctors who do higher risk operations but scrutinised to protect patients from unnecessary harm. My guess is that most patients wouldn't use it but would like to know it's there – just like having a tablet of Viagra on the bedside table. But the very act of publishing and comparing work with other units would make the staff raise their game.

Bristol

That's what I told the Bristol Heart Inquiry, anyway. Back in 1990, I went to the Edinburgh Fringe with Tony Gardner in a double act aiming to get away from traditional pun-laden, scatological medical humour. We were called Struck Off and Die. The show was called *Turn on to Your Left Hand Side, Draw Your Knees up to Your Chest and Take a Few Deep Breaths.*

By 1992, we'd collected a happy band of informants who fuelled the comedy. 'My local heart surgery unit's known as the Killing Fields and the Departure Lounge.' How we all laughed. The BBC made a CD of it.

I'd also started writing for *Private Eye* and met Steve Bolsin, the anaesthetist who told local doctors not to send children for heart surgery in Bristol. He convinced me babies were dying who would live if sent to Birmingham or Southampton. I asked people who'd worked on the unit if they'd allow their own babies to have heart surgery there. They said no. So I published audit figures from Bristol in the *Eye* with dark warnings not to go there.

Seven years later I'm summoned to the largest public inquiry in British history. You don't get a chance to opt out but I probably should have taken a lawyer. A shit-hot barrister skewered me from the off: 'When you referred to the Bristol unit as the Killing Fields and the Departure Lounge, that's medical humour, is it?'

A public inquiry is a tough gig. People haven't come to be entertained. I shat myself. After three hours in the witness box, there were thinly veiled threats of a custodial sentence if I didn't reveal all my sources. I was sent a pink letter saying that I might be publicly criticised for raising my concerns in a satirical magazine rather than through the correct channels. But when they did a paper chase of all the *Private Eye* articles, they'd found their way to all the correct channels, and nothing had been done. In 1992, audit wasn't compulsory, there were no agreed standards, the politicians neatly sidestepped any scandal and the medical establishment was only interested in the three As – alcohol, advertising and adultery.

Bristol was a great example of everything going wrong at every level. Lack of leadership, lack of political will, lack of insight, workaholism and everyone losing sight of the patients. The inquiry found that a third of children who underwent open heart surgery in Bristol between 1984 and 1995 received less than adequate care, and that between thirty and thirty-five babies died as a result. I'd like to think this has kick-started a focus on quality, safety and openness in the NHS but just about the only people collecting their results at the moment are heart surgeons and not all of them want to publish.

A few months after giving evidence at the inquiry and making lots of new friends at the Bristol Royal Infirmary, my stepfather had a heart attack, with severe triple vessel disease needing urgent heart surgery at our local unit. Bristol. I'd already lost one dad; to lose another would be careless. So I accompanied him on to the ward, with my list of awkward questions. Before I could get it out, a senior nurse spotted me and said to the professor of surgery, 'You know who that is, don't you? You'd better not fuck this one up.'

My second dad got excellent care because Bristol was well resourced and staffed by then. It gets excellent results for heart surgery and it publishes them. Whether it would have got there without the scandal is debatable. Probably not as quickly but with less trauma. At one stage in the inquiry, I thought one of the surgeons might kill himself. The Bristol parents took a heavy emotional hit; marriages dissolved and a few fathers committed suicide, partly out of guilt that they hadn't done the best for their children. Why didn't I know about Bristol if so many other people did? I'm not sure I did the right thing exposing it but I did. First as late-night medical humour, then anonymously in a satirical magazine and finally through desperate backtracking at a public inquiry. At least, as a journalist, I was forced to be accountable.

Beyond Bristol

In 1995, I was asked to present a show for BBC2 called *Trust Me, I'm a Doctor*. Each episode had a story where we'd highlight vast differences in the quality of NHS care. Doctors hated it. The *BMA News Review* called it *Trust Me, I'm a *****r*, so I knew we were on to something.

The worst-looking penis I've ever seen was not in the clap clinic but as the result of botched surgery for hypospadias, a condition where the hole in the penis is in the underside, not the end. At a specialist centre it's a two-stage operation to get it back to normal. I met a man who'd had fifty failed operations by a non-specialist. His penis looked like a butcher's dog had eaten it, and he was peeing out of five holes. He had to sit down to piss, he'd never had a sex life. But he kept going back to the same surgeon, out of loyalty.

Surgeons tend to make more high-profile errors than the rest of us but what amazed me was the number of them doing one or two really complex operations a year. They like the challenge and variety, and if you're an incredibly gifted surgeon, you may be able to do the odd thyroid, breast, aneurysm, kidney, oesophagus and liver. But if you only do the odd one, your results are statistically meaningless. Hardly a reason to continue.

For patients, the results of dabbling are anything but meaningless. We found surgeons 'having a go' at just about anything, no matter how complex, and getting disastrous results. Cleft lip repair, children's liver surgery, brain surgery, cancer surgery, orthopaedic surgery, endocrine surgery. If we hadn't highlighted the units doing it really well, it would have been very depressing.

There's still nothing to stop a surgeon attempting something way beyond his competence, if he (or she) lacks the insight to realise it. So long as he can find an anaesthetist to go along with it. Anaesthetists are the champions of patient safety. They have to be. A job that involves taking you as close to death as you can go, and then waking you up again, requires it. Anaesthetists have a high suicide rate, because they have self-doubt and access to good drugs. Surgeons have a much lower suicide rate. Because they are always right.

Whatever you've got, try to find a specialist centre with a support team that treats lots of people with your condition and publishes their results. Have a chat to the anaesthetist if you can. And trust your instincts. If something isn't right, try to get another opinion.

Simple but Deadly

Once you're in hospital, make sure you're fed and watered properly. People still die in the NHS through dehydration, fluid overload and starvation. Part of the problem is that the front-line staff are short on experience. Junior doctors now work far fewer hours in shifts, covering lots of wards they may not be familiar with. It's firefighting, twenty-four hours a day.

Cock-ups are surprisingly easy to make. We all put the CD back in the wrong case or type in the wrong PIN number at the cashpoint. Do it on intensive care and you kill someone. The NHS still hasn't embraced a culture of safety.

I've seen sassy patients and 'interfering' relatives who save lives by questioning the drug administration, sometimes mine. 'I don't normally have the pink ones'; 'They usually use a much smaller syringe'; and 'They normally put it in the drip bag, not straight into the vein.' Having an advocate makes a big difference, especially if your meal is put down just out of reach every evening. And then whisked away, untouched. 'Ooh, not hungry again, Albert?' And all because you're a messy eater.

And it's always worth asking everyone to wash their hands – staff, friends, the League of Friends trolley dolly trying to sell you a Mars bar when you're nil by mouth. 'Go on, I won't tell if you won't.'

Five thousand people a year die from hospital-acquired infection, made worse by new hospitals with too few beds packed to the rafters with patients in danger of breaching a waiting-time target. And your average doctor's white coat would trigger an air strike if it was found in Iraq.

GPs are just as filthy. One study found that only 15 per cent of us wash our thermometer in between patients. That's oral and rectal thermometers. Well, I've only got the one.

And if you go to your GP with an ear problem, he'll get out his otoscope and say, 'Ooh. There's a little bit of wax in there.' It's not your wax. Could be anyone's wax. So take in some sterile wipes for the instruments.

If you do opt for surgery, take a marker pen in with you too. You don't want any of that wrong kidney nonsense. And after the surgery, keep moving. We need the beds. Every year, someone's discovered snoring in the mortuary because we've been a bit hasty to judge.

I Think There's Something Wrong with Me
In 2001, I was writing a sitcom for BBC1 with Nigel Smith. The writing was going well, we were going to make a fortune and it would be sold to fifty-six countries. On 14 November, Nigel phoned me from a GP's waiting room to ask if Ramsay Hunt

syndrome was medical rhyming slang. He'd been to see a locum with numbness down the left side of the body and was told it would be better 'in a day or two'.

I hate being a doctor to my friends – it's really embarrassing when you get it wrong – but when Nigel said he had numbness down the left-hand side of his tongue, some vague neurological alarm bell went off. Jesus, that's brainstem, where all those vital things like breathing are controlled. Could be multiple sclerosis, could be a brain tumour, could be a stroke. Unlikely to be Ramsay Hunt. And we've got a sitcom to write. What do I say?

According to Nigel – and he's written a book about it so it must be true – I said, 'You're fucked, mate. Get a brain scan.' Just the response you'd expect from someone who's been a lecturer in communication skills at two UK medical schools. Nigel did eventually get to hospital and very nearly died. The fact that he didn't is partly down to his own bloody-mindedness and refusal to give up, the extraordinary love and tenacity of his wife and his good fortune to live in a country that will pay quarter of a million pounds on your health care without blinking.

I Think There's Something Wrong with Me is a comedy trauma and proof that with a partner like Michelle you can stand up to medical authority in the face of adversity. Nigel had a big mass in his brainstem, no one knew what it was; they wanted to do a needle biopsy to find out. This could damage him further and had a 5 per cent risk of death. On the plus side, they might find out what the diagnosis was. Michelle phoned me to ask my opinion, as a GP working in a clap clinic with no expertise in neurosurgery.

'Ask what the benefit is to Nigel. Will making the diagnosis make any difference to his prognosis? Or will it just make a better presentation at an international meeting?' Alas, whatever it was, it couldn't be removed – at least in the UK – so the biopsy was called off. Nigel already had fourteen UK experts on his case but then I remembered a neurosurgeon in New York called Patrick Kelly whom we'd featured on *Trust Me, I'm a Doctor* because he'd managed to remove brain tumours from NHS patients who'd been told they were inoperable. Was it worth getting a fifteenth opinion?

Michelle wanted it and she got it. The hospital wouldn't release the brain scans so she borrowed them and met Kelly at Heathrow Airport en route to accepting an award in Stockholm. He didn't think it was cancer, and even if it was, it wasn't operable.

To find out what the diagnosis was, you'll have to buy the book. It's a unique, and very funny, insight into the good (I'm alive) and bad (steroid psychosis, MRSA, guinea-pigging, treat you like a deaf imbecile) things that the NHS does to you in an attempt to get you better. And the BBC were very supportive about the sitcom. It was ditched after one series.

Getting Real about Death

We're all going to kick it sometime. But we're in denial about death. Some people won't even talk about it but I think it's the one area of our lives which could do with more medicalisation. I don't want to die when my brain's gone to putty and I'm soiling the bed in front of my kids. Fortunately, I don't have to, because I'm a doctor and in my bag I've got Dr Phil's Go Quickly Pills.

I know a few terminally ill doctors who've taken their morphine syringe up to the potting shed for a peaceful death. I've got a pact with Dr Rose. First one to put CDs in the toaster gets the pillow. If she can remember where she left it. Or what a pillow is. Never mind, there's always the syringe. Full of Marmite.

A lot of the resources that the NHS gobbles up are on people in their last throes of life. In our desperation not to be ageist, ITU is packed full of eighty-somethings who'll never be the same again. If we crack cancer and heart disease, we may get dementia instead. Patient choice will only ever mean anything if we can choose to die with dignity. I'm going to have 'Do Not Resuscitate' tattooed on my chest if I hit eighty. Or maybe sooner. I'll see how I feel.

Letting Go

When you die, let go of your organs. You can't take them with you. Three hundred people a year die for want of one of the organs we burn or bury. Clearly what happened at Alder Hey was unacceptable. There was an oddball putting heads in jars for his own amusement. There's probably the odd truck driver doing that. No profession's perfect. But the vast majority of pathologists do a good job, and a very important one if we ever want to get close to the truth about why people die.

As a junior doctor asking parents for post-mortems, I was complicit in the 'presumed' consent culture. I didn't have a clue which bits would be removed and so I was never in a position to tell the relatives. I just said, 'We'd like to perform a post-mortem to establish the precise cause of death so we can learn from it and benefit other patients.' Fifteen years ago I assumed, perhaps wrongly, that they didn't want a full inventory.

To me, the organ retention hysteria amounted to a realisation that pathologists collect pathology specimens. Big deal. Maybe this year we'll discover that surgeons cut you up with knives, bodies are left to rot underground and it gets pretty hot in the crematorium. Ironically, if we want to stop people dying prematurely, we need to get real about death. We're surrounded by it. You don't need to live next door to a leaky crematorium to inhale bits of the deceased. Every breath you take contains particles of the dearly departed.

Whether you want to know about what happens to you after death is a personal thing. Pathologists would remove, say, the liver and put in a brick to make up the weight. Take out a kidney and replace it with a packet of digestives. You don't bury Uncle Alf, you bury half man, half biscuit.

If anyone would like a piece of me after I die, you can take your pick. Just heckle your request. They're using dead skin for penis enlargements these days. That's an interesting angle for the afterlifers. I don't mind where I end up. Just please promise not to pursue my family asking if they want my bits back. Just bung what's left in a biodegradable bag and have a party.

Hands up if you want your organs to be used after death but only to keep someone else alive? . . . Most of you. Good. OK, hands up if you don't mind your bits being sold off for some sort of research? Hands up if you don't mind your bones being ground down for cosmetic surgery? Hands up if you don't mind your skin being used for penis enlargement? . . . Just you, madam. Hands up if you want your family to have some money for your dead bits? Most of us are worth far more dead than alive.

Post-mortem

There's an apocryphal story of a snide doctor saying to a desperate patient, 'I'm not entirely sure what the diagnosis is but I'm sure we'll find out at the post-mortem.' To which the patient replied, 'Anything, doctor – I'm even prepared to go private.' I'm not sure if BUPA offer a private PM service yet; for those who don't wish to rub shoulders with the hoi polloi in the mortuary, with £250-worth of screening tests thrown in. But I've always been a big fan of autopsies. They're the ultimate in quality control.

Or, put the other way round, if you want to cover something up and bury your mistakes, you don't order one. Half of what's written on the death certificate turns out to be tosh at post-mortem. Not even close to the truth. But without autopsies, we never know which half. Cancer is routinely misdiagnosed as heart disease and vice versa. Why did Shipman get away with it for so long? In our new 'open, honest, learn from your mistakes' NHS, you'd expect surgeons and physicians to be beating down the mortuary doors to find out how their patients really died and what they can do to improve practice in the future. But alas, PMs are at an all-time low. Let's bring them back. But only when we've died.

Feedback

Before you die, try to give some feedback. The NHS can only improve if you get involved. We need to know when we've cocked up; we need to know when we've done something good. Try to give positive points first. Marriage guidance counsellors say you need five positives for every negative for a relationship to thrive.

So, accentuate the positive and think the NHS better. Hug your doctor whenever you can – he or she needs love as much as you do. Trust me, he'd love to be kissed full on the mouth. Or is that just me?

Have we saved the NHS? Who knows? But I'd urge you to take an evolutionary perspective on this. We're just interlopers in the geological nanosecond. We're here, we're gone. That's it. This is as good as it gets. There's no almighty master, no grand design, no great purpose. We're just African apes on a very brief joyride.

If you hold hands with your mum who holds hands with her mum who holds hand with her mum, in under a mile you'll get back to your ape ancestor.

If you live in Wales, it's about fifty feet.

So let's enjoy life. If you feel fine, don't go to your GP. We can only make you worse. Get out and have a blast. You only go round the track once. Bollocks to doctors.

However, if you do get sick, I would recommend a copy of my book, *Trust Me, I'm a Doctor*. You don't have to read it. If you're too scared to stand up to the system, or you're bleeding profusely, just wave the book at the staff. It might just save your life.

Signed copies available in the foyer. And dedications: 'Dear Auntie Maud, good luck with the bowel resection.' And I'll also be available for some after-show hugging, two at a time.

If you don't fancy that, there is one other thing more powerful than even my Love Tablet, guaranteed to save you in times of crisis. First we need to stand up, hold hands and start a love train, just like the O'Jays suggested, based on the best available evidence at the time. And here he is. I give you . . . Pope John Paul Jimmy Savile Mullet II . . .

All you have to do is believe.

Goodnight.

GLORIA

'How was Burkina Faso?'

'Still landlocked. But you've got some tough competition out there.'

'Any more Dr Phils?'

'Sadly not. No gingers either.'

'That's something. What did you make of the book?'

'Some of the content worked for me. Not sure about the production values. I wasn't expecting you to publish it yourself.'

'A few people are interested if I can raise my profile a bit.'

'When are you next on *Countdown*?'

'September.'

'Too late. And I'm not sure I like the talking to the audience bit.'

'It's a transcript of a show. That's what I do.'

'Yes, but it tends to confuse if you're reading it.'

'I'm not doing any more photocopying. Any more news on the judging panel?'

'Alastair Campbell's in.'

'I've met him. We were both sucking the corporate cock.'

'The same one?'

'Yes, in front of lots of angry rheumatologists. He couldn't believe how much doctors whinge. Reckons you've got to be a lot more intelligent to get your message across.'

'He said that?'

'Just make some link, however tenuous, with what you think needs to happen to the NHS and what politicians think needs to happen. Then you're seen as part of the solution and not just another moaner.'

'How much do you think you're to blame for the state of the NHS?'

'Me personally?'

'You campaigned to reduce junior doctors' hours. Politicians listened. The hours were halved and now there isn't enough training.'

'European law reduced the hours but we haven't doubled the doctors. So hospitals are covered by the bare minimum of staff, on their own. Hardly good training or safe medicine.'

'We are producing more doctors.'

'Without enough training posts for them to go to. And thanks to the sham application process, some of the best doctors were frozen out.'

'Welcome to Planet Earth. Consultants have blocked their own expansion for years. They all want a slice of the private cake.'

'Private medicine is less of an issue now waiting lists have come down.'

'Labour's got something right then. And there'll be more jobs for juniors when the overseas doctors are sent packing.'

'British graduates don't want dead-end non-consultant jobs.'

'Tough. We can't afford more consultants. They're too expensive. Doctors have priced themselves out of the market with their amazing pay deals.'

'Consultants are only being paid for all the hours they used to put in for free. And you can't blame GPs for hitting targets the government set for them and then claiming the agreed payment.'

'The Department of Health negotiators cocked up, big time.'

'The BMA are hardly brilliant negotiators. It makes you wonder how much the private sector has fleeced the NHS if the negotiating is that soft.'

'Why aren't doctors happy if they're earning more?'

'Because we've sold our souls. Taken the money in return for having our lives controlled by targets we don't all agree with. And then we're made scapegoats for the debt.'

'That's also your fault. You exposed the Bristol heart scandal, you told the public inquiry that doctors couldn't be trusted to regulate themselves so now the government's doing it for them.'

'I said doctors couldn't be trusted to regulate themselves in secret. The NHS was completely unaccountable and now it's a bit less so. But I didn't say the government should force reforms on the staff that don't have any evidence base. I still believe in treating according to need, not target.'

'And you invited al-Qaeda into the NHS.'

'No, I didn't.'

'You said, in 2002, "The NHS is so vast and unaccountable, nobody will ever track you down. And it's great if you need to lie low for a while. As I was saying to Dr bin Laden, only the other day." That's a clear invitation to infiltrate.'

'It was a gag.'

'Do you want to be taken seriously or not? *Take a Break* want you to write a piece about what Gordon Brown should do with the NHS.'

'Do I have to?'

'Yes. You need to raise your profile and sound authoritative. Colonic irrigation was a disaster. You sound ridiculous. The poet's a bit flaky but she could be good for the healing arts angle. Is she attractive?'

'I can't remember.'

'I've put a call through to Dervla Kirwan's agent, just in case. Tuberculosis was just about useable but you didn't seem to know your stuff.'

'But that's what I preach. Patients are the experts in their illnesses. They can find out far more about their condition than I can.'

'Yes, yes, yes. But we could do with at least a few consultations where you appear to know what you're talking about without consulting Dr Google. I've asked the nurse to set you up with some nits.'

'I know nothing about nits. The nit nurse does all that.'

'Our research suggests people who watch Channel 4 worry more about nits than cancer, obesity and heart disease combined. If you can pull off a good consultation, it could really shoot you up the rankings.'

'When's she coming?'

'Tomorrow. And I've booked you in for a school drug talk too. We're adding a "good with children" round.'

'Super.'

'You've got twelve hours to turn yourself into the World's Most Knowledgeable Nit and Solvent Doctor.'

ELLIE

'Doctor, it's a disaster. Ellie's got head lice.'

'So did the Ancient Egyptians.'

'What?'

'They've found nits on mummies.'

'Are nits the same as head lice?'

'If you'd asked me yesterday, I'd have said yes. But no, nits are the old hatched eggs of the head louse, a cuddly wingless insect called *Pediculus capitis*.'

'I've got one in this jar.'

'Excellent, Ellie. Let's have a look at it, shall we? You have the magnifying glass and I'll get it in my forceps. This is quite a big one, oval in shape and a bit pointed at each end, wouldn't you say?'

'Stop it, Dr Hammond.'

'It's an insect, so how many legs does it have, Ellie?'

'Six?'

'Five. One's come off in the forceps. And a stretchy, flabby body which allows it to take in lots of food. And what does it eat, Ellie?'

'Plankton?'

'That's right. Your blood.'

'Yes, all right.'

'It doesn't move very quickly but then it doesn't need to because it's hiding away in your hair, like an animal in the jungle. Oh look, it's dropped a faecal pellet. See, Ellie? It's done a little pooh. She's got some eggs here which are only just a bit bigger than a full stop but they're pale brown which makes them hard to see against Ellie's hair.'

'How fascinating.'

'When they're freshly laid, the light passes through them so you can actually see the colour of the hair through the eggs. Ellie, let me look at your hair. It's lovely and clean.'

'They like that, don't they?'

'To be honest, they'll go for any hair that's got blood underneath. Now, Ellie's got loads of nits, glistening white in her hair. They're actually quite beautiful.'

'No they're not.'

'When the mother louse lays an egg, she sticks it firmly onto the hair using a home-made Superglue, which sets instantly. It hatches in a week, or sooner on a warm head if you run around and get sweaty.'

'Does that mean I shouldn't do PE?'

'Nice try. The baby louse inside breaks through the membrane, sucks in air and passes it through its backside to the tune of "There's No Business Like Show Business".'

'Really?'

'Yes, apart from the Ethel Merman. So the back end of the egg fills up with air pressure and that forces the little louse forward till it pushes off the cap at the top and explodes out.'

'And then it sucks my blood?'

'Yes. It puts its proboscis into your scalp, feels around for a blood vessel and then pumps in saliva to stop the blood clotting on the way up.'

'Cool.'

'I think your father's fainted.'

'Cool.'

'Now I'm going to use a fine-toothed plastic comb to search for lice. They shed their skin three times before becoming an adult.'

'How long do they live for?'

'Thirty days tops but usually less because you scratch them and wash them away. Also, the mums tend to get stuck in their own egg glue, which isn't pleasant.'

'How many eggs does she lay?'

'About half a dozen for a few days, then she slowly tails off to one or two.'

'So she's born by sucking air in through her bum, loses her skin three times, has babies every day for a month and then dies.'

'If she's lucky.'

'What a life.'

'She can't swim either.'

'When would she have time to learn?'

'In water she goes into suspended animation, closing everything down and waiting until the conditions get better. Head lice can hold their breath longer than almost anything else on earth but their skins aren't thick enough to stop the water getting in so eventually they turn into bloated balloons with their legs stuck out in all directions.'

'They're almost human then.'

'We share a lot of the same DNA. Now if you wet your hair, the lice stay still, which is very convenient if you want to comb them off your head.'

'I'm not sure I do now. Will they do me any harm?'

'Mainly socially.'

'Is it true that if you break their legs they can't lay eggs?'

'No. Eggs don't come out of legs. Don't they teach you anything these days?'

'Will I pass them on to my friends?'

'You can. But head lice don't jump or fly so you can only do it by touching heads and letting them walk across.'

'So if I don't lock horns with anyone, I could just keep my lice?'

'Yes. It depends how much you hate bug busting. Some

families pretend it's quality time together but usually it ends up with stressed, overanxious parents spilling cheap conditioner on the carpet and being really rough with your tangles.'

'Thank you, Dr Phil.'

'Thank you, Ellie. Wake your father up on the way out.'

ALI

'Hello, Ali. Good to see you again.'

'I've read your book.'

'Did you like it?'

'It was all right. Bit repetitive.'

'It hasn't been edited yet.'

'Have you got a publication date?'

'No. I'm hoping my old publisher might take it. They did *Trust Me, I'm a Doctor* but it's out of print.'

'That good?'

'Ahead of its time.'

'Was it an ironic title?'

'Yes.'

'You've written two books, both about standing up to doctors, one of which is now out of print?'

'So what can I do for you?'

'Are you recording this?'

'Yes. According to the jaundiced receptionist with the low-set ears, you've signed a consent form. She says "thanks", by the way.'

'For what?'

'Picking up her jaundice. Gallstones.'

'Isn't that confidential?'

'She wanted you to know. And she's given you some chutney.'

'How lovely.'

'Not really. Someone with shingles gave it to me, and I passed it on.'

'I've got a poem for you.'

'I see.'

'No, you don't.'

'No, I don't. Why have you brought me a poem?'

'Three reasons. Your book inspired me, and I thought it would be more interesting for you to spend ten minutes discussing poetry than peering at my cervix or whatever you're being bribed to do this week.'

'And?'

'I'd like it to be performed on TV by Dervla Kirwan.'

'That's not quite what I had in mind. These consultations are supposed to demonstrate a shift in the balance of power between doctor and patient, as advocated in my books.'

'So if I want to read a poem I can?'

'I suppose. What's the third reason?'

'I'd like to be your poet in residence.'

'Mine?'

'The practice's. There's a big "arts in health care" movement out there. Poetry helps patients and staff make sense of their experience. As your book says.'

'I'll put it to the partners.'

'Do you write poetry?'

'Occasionally.'

'What was the first poem you ever wrote?'

'Can't remember.'

'Try.'

'When I was a medical student, I wrote a poem called "Jobs".'

'About house jobs?'

'Not really.'

'How did it go?'

'Sometimes when I have a poo/It cuts off nice and clean/So when I check the paper/I can't tell that I've been . . .'

'Is that it?'

'No. I was giving you a get-out pause.'

'I think I've got the flavour of it.'

'I remember asking my GP tutor to put it to music but he declined on the grounds that it was unbelievably puerile.'

'I'm with him on that. Anything else?'

'I once wrote a poem to a writer called Isabel Losada, who I met on a package holiday to the Gambia. She reminded me of it twenty years later.'

'Is it a love poem?'

'I'm not convinced. "You've got rubber lips/Your teeth stick out/Your tits aren't much/To write home about/So why do I like you?"'

'Would you like to read one of my poems instead?'

'Yes, I think that would be better.'

'If you murder it, I'll kill you.'

'"Hippo Crates". Is that the title?'

'Yes.'

'Not Hippocrates?'

'No.'

"Governments ignore their pleas
For funding never meets their needs
Short on numbers, under siege
Yet swore to make you better

Swapping hearts and squelching pox
Round the clock they never stop
There's good and bad, a bit like cops
All swore to make you better

No one questions the dedication
To years of study and privation
Required to reach the lofty station
That swore to make you better

Say someday health gets ripped asunder
You soon might well begin to wonder
If you aren't just a number
They swore to make you better

One more ticked off, this case is closed
Another patient diagnosed
Take four of these and one of those
We swore to make you better

Now hear me, Doc, I'm less than thrilled
To be simply gobbling pills
Prescribing drugs takes little skill
You swore to make me better

Blank looks, cross frowns, a roll of eyes
I will speak up, don't act surprised,
Despite the fact I well realise
Who swore to make me better

We know it's tough and time is short
But those you see are sick and fraught
So treat with kindness, act with thought
I swear it makes it better . . ."

'That's brilliant. Very challenging.'
    'Thank you. Now let *me* read it.'
    'Sorry, did I murder it?'
    'I'd just like to read it to you. You can lie on the couch if you like.'
    'Why would I do that?'
    'It'll be more powerful. Lie on the couch and close your eyes.'
    'No.'

'You're so uptight. You want to come across as interesting, don't you?'

'Yes.'

'And your book advocates opening up to art.'

'Yes, but not to temporary residents.'

'What happened to "hug me, I'm a doctor"?'

'Not lying-down hugs.'

'You could do with losing a bit of control. Open your third eye.'

'I can't. It's clenched tight.'

'You wrote that art can take you to another place, give you another perspective.'

'I think that was complementary therapy.'

'Complementary therapy is art. That's why it works. Now breathe deeply and focus on every word.'

'Then you'll leave me alone for ever?'

'No.'

'Do you still want your cholesterol checked?'

'Shut up. I'm turning the tape off.'

MATTHEW

'Hello, have a seat. I've got a note from Sister about bedbugs.'

'She said you were the expert.'

'Since last night, yes. Show me what you've got.'

'I just woke up with them.'

'They look like bites. Just on your left arm?'

'Pretty much. I've got a few on my feet.'

'Does your bed smell of almonds?'

'Is this relevant?'

'Possibly.'

'Possibly.'

'And have you noticed any sooty trails on your bedposts or sheets? Like a fountain pen leaking ink?'

'Yes, I have actually.'

'*Cimex lectularius.*'

'What?'

'I agree with Sister. Bedbugs.'

'So my wife's been unfaithful again?'

'I've no idea but they're not sexually transmitted. At the end of the nineteenth century, 75 per cent of houses in Britain had bedbugs. And young gentlemen on the Grand Tour would take a piglet with them in their coach. When they arrived at a hotel, they'd stick the pig in their bed and then go downstairs and have supper. When they came back, the bed was warmed and bedbugs were fed. So they had a good night's sleep.'

'Why are you telling me this?'

'To sound informed.'

'Do bedbugs kill?'

'Only through worry. They're lovely-looking beasts, about eight millimetres long with a short head, prominent antennae and dark, compound eyes. They live in the frame of your bed and come out at night to bite you with their slender, rotating mouthparts.'

'Too much information.'

'Having located a blood vessel, they suck like buggery until their chestnut brown bodies swell up to twice the size and they turn purple.'

'Are you sure this is what I've got?'

'No. We'd need to catch one and they're really hard to spot.'

'Why?'

'They're brown and hide in wood.'

'How did they get there?'

'From bats or birds originally but humans have more blood and we can't fly away so naturally they selected us. Ah, here are some photos.'

'No thanks.'

'Those sausage-shaped ones have had a good meal but the hungry ones are oval and flat. Cute, eh?'

'I've never seen one of them biting me.'

'They're actually quite lazy and only feed once every couple of months. If you're in bed and they don't have to move too far, they crawl out of your bed frame just before dawn.'

'How do they know I'm in bed?'

'They start by detecting the carbon dioxide in your breath and then track you through warmth.'

'But why have they only bitten my arm?'

'They don't like going under the bedclothes, so they only bite the bits that hang out of the bed. Often just an arm or a foot or, if you've got ginger hair, a penis.'

'Why don't I feel the bite?'

'Bedbugs are very considerate. They bite delicately and suck gently.'

'Has the same bug given me all of these?'

'No. You must have loads. Which is why I asked you about ink spots on your sheets.'

'What are they caused by?'

'Bug pooh. Mainly water and digested blood.'

'Mine?'

'Or your wife's. The droplets dry down to star-shaped sooty spots. They're quite beautiful in close-up.'

'And the almonds?'

'That's just in extreme situations. Loads of bugs make a sweet sickly smell in your bed, a bit like when you use marzipan for foreplay.'

'Won't they just die out eventually?'

'Unlikely. If you keep feeding them, they'll keep having sex. While you're asleep, the male inserts his enormous phallus through the side of the female's abdomen. The sperm then swim through the blood of the female to find the oviduct and penetrate the eggs.'

'That's it. I'm off to Argos.'

'The stuff you buy in shops just winds them up. It doesn't kill them.'

'What does?'

'The Bed Bug Man.'

'Don't be absurd.'

'OK. Integrated Pest Management Services. They pitch up at your house with overalls, respirators and a big bag of insecticides.'

'So the neighbours know you're unclean?'

'The Bed Bug Man is trained to deal with your shock, horror, disgust, denial and feelings low self-esteem in a highly professional manner.'

'But it's a quick squirt of DDT and they're out?'

'No. They'll sign you up to a programme of compulsive hoovering. But before DDT, the only way to deal with a heavy infestation was to hack the house back to the brickwork, remove all the plaster and go over all the surfaces with a blow torch.'

'But insecticides will kill them?'

'They did. So the bugs evolved resistance. Numbers are at a fifteen-year high.'

'What if I move house?'

'Don't take the furniture. Second-hand wood is full of bugs. And don't go on holiday either. In the centres of large cities, hotels are chock-full of bugs which you then bring back in your luggage. They're the best-travelled occupants of the planet.'

'What if we leave home for a month, starve the bastards out and then come back?'

'No good. They can live in your house for four months without a meal, just waiting for your return. They survived the insecticide purges of the fifties and sixties and came out laughing.'

'So I'm stuffed?'

'Relax. Everyone's got an unexplained bite or two, if you look closely enough. Get a bed pig, napalm your house or go live in the tepee. Or just let yourself be bitten every few months. You decide. It's called patient choice. Now go home.'

ST AUGUSTINE'S

'Hello, everyone. I'm Dr Hammond, I'm a local GP and TV personality, and I've been invited to talk to you about drugs. Or rather answer your questions. So fire away. Yes. Catrina?'

'Catriona.'

'Sorry.'

'Have you been on *Countdown*?'

'Twenty four times.'

'Do you actually do any medicine these days?'

'Every Thursday. Any questions at all about drugs? Yes, you. Will, is it?'

'Is it true that they record a whole week of *Countdown* in one day?'

'Yes.'

'So you've only actually done it for less than five days?'

'We lost one programme to the Cheltenham Festival.'

'What do you do for the rest of the year?'

'Anyone with any vaguely drug-related question?'

'If I take drugs, will I end up as leader of the Conservative Party?'

'Possibly. Or in the Cabinet. But only if you try them once and pretend not to enjoy them.'

'Does all glue make you high, or just some types?'

'A lot of them do. Anything that's a solvent that gives off a vapour can be inhaled but I wouldn't recommend it.'

'What about Pritt sticks?'

'No, they don't give off a vapour, which is why you have them in school.'

'Can you name the glues that do?'

'I can't remember the names but it's illegal to sell solvents to people who you think are going to inhale them.'

'My sister sniffs hairspray. And air freshener. Says it's like being pissed.'

'And what's that like?'

'You should know, you're a doctor.'

'Has anyone else got a question?'

'Can you sniff petrol?'

'You could. But it would probably make you sick.'

'It gives me the giggles. Lighter refills are good too. And felt-tips.'

'Over sixty people die each year from—'

'Felt-tips? I don't believe you, doctor.'

'From all solvents.'

'How?'

'Fred Dinenage, Jack Hargreaves, Jon Miller and Bunty James.'

'What?'

'I was harking back to a golden age when children were amused with science, history, maths and simple puzzles.'

'What's he on?'

'Solvents can kill by heart attack or suffocation in the plastic bag you've put over your head to trap the vapour. Or you can squirt it down your throat until it stops you breathing. Or you can hallucinate and dive off a building or jump in front of a train. Long-term abuse of solvents damages the brain, liver and kidneys.'

'Yeah, yeah, yeah. But of all the thousands of kids who sniff, a very small number of them die, right?'

'True, but you can never be sure how it will affect you.'

'Do you get hooked?'

'Not really. But you can get a shocking headache and a hangover and a nasty rash around your mouth. And it makes you tired and dopey and you do badly at school.'

'And is it illegal?'

'No. Can I go now?'

'One more question, doctor.'

'Yes, Will?'

'What drugs have you taken, recently and in the past?'

'Australian Shiraz.'

'Is that it?'

'No.'

WHAT SHOULD GORDON DO?

What should Gordon Brown do with the NHS? The great con of Blair's reform was to preach the rhetoric of patient power whilst handing over control, and a vast sum of public money, to the private sector. To argue that this is not privatisation of the NHS is nonsense but then Blair excelled at that.

Clearly a return to the old Labour Stalinism of diktat by bureaucracy is unwise. And yet Blair's model is equally didactic, suggesting market competition is the only way forward and peppering it with promises of choice, when people only get to choose what the government wants them to.

Brown must reverse this without seeming to be old Labour. The solution is to deliver what Blair pretended to promise: 'a devolved NHS where 80 per cent of the decisions are made locally'. If Labour really wants patients to get involved in shaping services, it has to move the money upstream and stop the dysfunctional schism between top-down marketing and local decision making.

Social networks are essential for health and the NHS would fall to pieces without all the work done by support groups. So support and expand them. Age Concern provides home care services, the Alzheimer's Society gives you more support than the NHS, and Arthritis Care and the Expert Patient Programme can teach you how to manage your illnesses far better than I can. The trick is to focus on what keeps you well, rather than waiting for the NHS to swallow you up when you're sick.

So what happens in the NHS if the staff and patients are freed from central control and allowed to think creatively?

Football Therapy

Janette Hynes, an occupational therapist at East London and City Mental Health Trust, uses football to help patients with severe mental illness whilst in hospital but they had no team to play with when they got out. Despite resistance from the prevailing attitudes in mainstream football, she set up the Positive Mental Attitude League (PMAL) in 2002, using her expertise as a professional footballer.

The PMAL now has fourteen teams, with twenty waiting to join, and has demonstrated better physical and mental health for its players. Many have lost the flab, stopped smoking and got jobs. The league links with social services. Men and plenty of women love their football and if they don't turn up to training, it's a good predictor of relapse that can be picked up quickly.

Pathology Therapy

Sue Morgan, a clinical nurse specialist at St James's Hospital, Leeds, looks after children and teenagers with cancer. One of them asked her, 'What colour is my cancer?' So she set up a service where young patients can view their cancer under a microscope. It's had huge psychological benefits. Many children (and adults) imagine their cancer as a ravenous beast, all hooded, black and menacing, eating away at them. In reality, their cancers looked like 'sausages', 'Granny's wallpaper' and 'jelly beans'. Far from trivialising their illness, it's given the children confidence to fight it. A side-effect has been that pathologists have started talking to patients again. This could easily be rolled out across the NHS.

Going Public

Death rates have come down since heart surgeons have published their figures, with no evidence that sicker patients are being denied surgery. In a paper in *Heart* (January 2007), Ben

Bridgewater and colleagues in Manchester looked at 26,000 patients who underwent heart bypass operations between 1997 and 2005. Public disclosure of death rates began in 2001, after the Bristol Inquiry. The death rate for coronary artery bypass graft (CABG) patients after public disclosure was significantly lower than it had been before, falling from 2.4 per cent to 1.8 per cent. However, the predicted death rate steadily rose from 3 per cent to 3.5 per cent, suggesting that more complicated cases or elderly patients were being taken on. So publishing results and giving patients informed consent may have the added benefit of making surgical teams 'up their game'. Or perhaps the technology has just got better year on year. Either way, there's no reason why publication shouldn't extend into other specialties. And patients may finally be able to make decisions based on competence rather than car parking.

ME for Kids
Esther Crawley is a consultant paediatrician in Bath specialising in children with ME. One in 100 get it badly enough to stop them accessing school (it's the commonest cause of long-term school absence, ahead of leukaemia). And contrary to popular prejudice, it's more common amongst the poor (they just suffer in silence). ME is part genetic, part environmental (virus or head injury), and children typically have memory and concentration problems, feel knackered after exertion and have unrefreshing sleep. They can also get pain just about anywhere (head, stomach, joints). Despite a wealth of evidence demonstrating its existence, only one in ten children get treatment.

Dr Crawley has developed a regional service, trains other doctors, goes into schools and social services, supports parents, works with charities and spreads the message through the media. But the key to her success is allowing the children to work out and manage their own rehabilitation programmes.

Children hate being ill, they want to get better and they do. As Crawley puts it, 'In 80 per cent of the cases, the child makes the diagnosis before the GP. I advise them to ask for tests and referral.' So children with ME, one of the most ignored and vilified illnesses of recent years, make their diagnosis, get referred, help design their rehabilitation programmes and achieve full recovery 90 per cent of the time. The message is clear: use the creativity of professionals to free patients to make informed decisions and sort themselves out. And it might save the NHS.

'What do you think, Gloria?'

'Vigorously uplifting. Just right for *Take a Break*. You've taken your own advice, accentuated the positive and touched on a way forward for the NHS.'

'Not very funny though, is it?'

'We don't want funny doctors, we want inspiring, positive ones. The Ginger Whinger is dead.'

'No he isn't. He's just resting. I think the poetry helped.'

'Ali's?'

'Mine. She asked me to start writing and I can't stop. It's invigorating. Would you like to hear one?'

'If you must.'

'"Terribly attractive to women—"'

'That's enough. You still haven't shown me your early stand-up.'

'I don't want to revisit it. It's very negative. And it makes me anxious.'

'Because of what you went through?'

'And what it did to me. And I don't think it's relevant now.'

'More relevant than your poems. On my desk by Monday, please. And how are you getting on with the nurse referrals?'

'It's a lot of homework. I sound knowledgeable but I think we're going too much the other way.'

'Information overload?'

'Yes. Can I go back to therapeutic bullshit with a dash of Dr Google?'

'All right. We've nearly got enough anyway. We need one or two showing some anger management though.'

'Why?'

'We want to see if you can get out of a tight spot.'

'What if I don't have any angry patients?'

'Make some. Now what are we going to do about your nose hair?'

DAVID

'Hello, I'm Dr Hammond.'

'Where's Dr Fanners?'

'He had to retire, I'm afraid. Have a seat.'

'But he was, what, mid fifties?'

'Can you imagine what thirty years of full-time general practice does to the human brain?'

'He was a great GP. Did he have a good send-off?'

'It was fairly low-key. And against his will. Anyway, I'm seeing some of his patients until they find a replacement.'

'So you aren't the replacement?'

'No, I'm Thursdays only.'

'Why?'

'Because I don't want to end up like Dr Fanners.'

'But you've got my records?'

'Yep. And you deserve a "loyal customer" badge. This is your twentieth visit to the doctor this year.'

'How do you know?'

'The computer. I press control-shift-A next to your name and it gives the number of attendances.'

'Why would you need to know that?'

'Well, on average men of your age attend twice a year, so either you must be pretty sick or . . .'

'Or?'

'Or there's a complex web of psychosocial issues triggering your attendance.'

'I want antibiotics.'

'Why?'

'I've got a cold and I feel like shit.'

'I see.'

'Good. So if you'll let me have them, I'll leave you in peace with control-shift-A.'

'Why do you think you need antibiotics?'

'Because I've got a cold and I feel like shit. Are you deaf?'

'It's just that I don't give antibiotics for feeling shit. Or colds.'

'Well, perhaps you could explain why Dr Fanners always gave me antibiotics and I always got better.'

'It's called association. Ninety-nine percent of drivers involved in car accidents are wearing shoes. Does that mean that wearing shoes makes you crash the car? Would you ban shoes on the strength of it?'

'Why was Dr Fanners forced out?'

'He had a car crash. Wearing shoes and with five times the legal limit of alcohol in his blood. I don't think he'll be back.'

'Shame. You could always get an appointment, he was always on time and you were in and out in under two minutes.'

'With a prescription?'

'If you wanted one. Aren't you supposed to offer patients choice?'

'Only if it's good for them. You would have got better from your colds just as quickly without the antibiotics. Trust me.'

'You think you're so clever, don't you?'

'Well, doctors are in the top 0.1 per cent of the academic population.'

'If you're so clever, perhaps you could explain why I always got antibiotics from Dr Fanners, who I presume was also in the top nought point one per cent of the academic population.'

'Not towards the end he wasn't.'

'What?'

'Dr Fanners trained in an era when antibiotics were seen as cure-alls. Magic bullets, if you like. And despite the overwhelming evidence that they don't make a jot of difference to viral infections, he preferred to stick with his beliefs. Now I'm not saying he was a bad doctor, far from it, but medical science progressed rather faster than he did.'

'Are you being a patronising arsehole on purpose?'

'Yes. I need to record a consultation with a bit of anger in it.'

'Well, you've succeeded.'

'And I understand your anger. You and generations before you have had your faith in a pill for every ill reinforced by Dr Fanners and his idiosyncratic prescribing. But I'm saying let's challenge those beliefs, let's break free from the drug culture and let's give your body a chance to heal itself.'

'I'm not leaving without my banana syrup. I can't swallow tablets.'

'You're twenty-seven and you can't swallow tablets?'

'No.'

'Hang on. I'll just add that to your records. T-w-e-n-t-y-s-e-v-e-n a-n-d s-t-i-l-l c-a-n'-t s-w-a-l-l-o-w t-a-b-l-e-t-s.'

'Do you have to?'

'Yes. For safety reasons. Now I'd love to take you to banana heaven but your cold is caused by a rhinovirus that lives inside the cells of your respiratory epithelium where antibiotics can't get to it. Prescribing would merely reinforce your doctor-dependence, undermine your autonomy and promote resistance.'

'You've got about three seconds left before I punch your lights out.'

'Now you're just being childish. I'm trying to educate you. Antibiotics don't cure colds or flu, and they aren't much use for tonsillitis and ear infections either. To get penicillin out of me, you'd need to come back with syphilis.'

'Can I at least have a photo of Carol Vorderman?'

'If you promise not to punch me. Here you go.'

'I've already got that one.'

'Tough.'

GRANT

'Hello. I've had a bit of tummy trouble.'

'There's a lot of it about.'

'So I went to see the grumpy old GP.'

'Dr Fanners?'

'Yes. But I couldn't get in to see him today.'

'He's gardening for life.'

'Anyway, he said—'

'It's probably a virus.'

'Shut up and let me finish. He said I had "Query Appendicitis".'

'To you?'

'No, in the letter I took to hospital. "Dear Surgeon. This irritating 'man' complains bitterly of right-sided abdominal pain. Query Appendicitis."'

'Well, it serves you right for opening it.'

'Aren't I allowed to read my letters?'

'Only if we've censored the insults.'

'Well, I wasn't happy about Query Appendicitis. Is that the same as gay bowel syndrome?'

'No. Gay bowel syndrome is a presumptive medical term for symptoms that can result from anal penetration – pain, bleeding, infection, poor wind control – irrespective of the sex of the recipient. "Query Appendicitis" means that Dr Fanners thought you might have appendicitis but wasn't sure. It's normally written as "?Appendicitis".'

'Shouldn't that be "?Appendicitis?"?'

'Perhaps. But too may queries can look as if the doctor

knows nothing, rather than not a lot. So we tend to economise.'

'Tell me. I had to wait four hours for a doctor, six hours for a bed and when I finally got one, there was no pillow. The only thing they didn't economise on was the internals. I was hurting in my right lower abdomen, not my rectum, so why put me through that?'

'That's an interesting point. Most doctors were brought up with the aphorism "If you don't put your finger in it, you'll put your foot in it."'

'It felt like it.'

'Meaning that it's easy to miss something important. For example, most rectal cancers occur within a finger reach.'

'So they were checking if I had cancer?'

'No, in your case they were checking to see if you had an inflamed appendix in a pelvic position, which would make the rectum tender high up on the right-hand side.'

'It was after the fifth time.'

'That's teaching hospitals for you. To be fair, there are realistic plastic models of the pelvis that allow medical students to feel a rectal growth or a large craggy prostate without troubling real patients but alas there's no model that says, "Ooh it hurts, doctor." "Where?" "High up on the left-hand side." "Your left or my left?" "Your left. My right." "Well, actually I'm behind you, so your right is my right and your left is my left. So which is it?" "Hang on. Let me think . . ." "Would you like a cigarette?" "You have one of mine, doctor – they're in my trousers." "Which pocket?" "Right." "Are you sure?" etc.'

'But why do it at all? I felt grotty, I was flushed, I was off my food, I had a temperature, it hurt to move, my tummy was acutely tender over my appendix – it was fairly obvious I had appendicitis.'

'And did you?'

'No. But the point is that I was sick enough to need opening up under anaesthetic without being sullied while I was still awake.'

'Most doctors don't think internal examinations are necessary in the diagnosis of appendicitis but they might do it to rule out something else like bleeding.'

'Him and his four mates. And even then, they got it wrong.'

'Well, it's a very difficult diagnosis to make. Half of those who are told they have appendicitis don't and half that are told they don't, do.'

'They told me mine looked normal but they took it out anyway and sent it to the lab. And the lab said the tip was inflamed but not infected.'

'That's because the surgeon will have squeezed it with his forceps to try to trick the pathologist into thinking it really was appendicitis and he hasn't opened you up for no reason.'

'Well, they said all my internal organs looked healthy, so I suppose that's something.'

'And what did they say the diagnosis was?'

'They weren't sure. The letter they gave me to give to you says "Appendix Normal ?Viral".'

'See, I told you.'

'Smug git.'

'Don't mention it.'

ALI

'Hello Ali.'

'Hi. How did you get on?'

'Fine thanks. I've written three already.'

'That was quick.'

'I know. Creatively, I'm on fire.'

'No buck teeth, tits or poo?'

'Not a sausage. They're not medical either. I've taken your advice and looked elsewhere for my muse.'

'Good.'

'I'm not sure if they are.'

'I'm not expecting Keats.'

'Do you want to see them?'

'I want you to read them to me.'

'Do I have to?'

'Yes. It's my turn to lie down. Shall I take my shoes off?'

'If you wouldn't mind. "Terribly attractive—"'

'I'm not ready yet.'

'Sorry.'

'Sorry about the socks.'

'"Terribly attractive—"'

'Is that the title?'

'No, it's the first line. It doesn't have a title. None of them do.'

'That's OK.'

"Terribly attractive
To women

He tried
And proving
Proved that women
Were more than
His idea of a woman
Waiting and wanting
But they lie alone
And
In joining
All that can be proved
Is a mutual loneliness
A craving
Not to be stopped in an us
But in an alone thought . . .”

'I've finished.'

'Oh, right.'

'Go easy on me. Positive points first, then constructive criticisms.'

'Carry on.'

'Don't you want to discuss it?'

'I'd like to hear all three first.'

"Reach
And touch
I'm here
I know the you
That crying
Needs
So we've not met
For too long
And too many rumours
But reach
And I'll catch the real in you

And the other
The artifice
Will flow
Through my arms
Leaving only you
And me . . .”

'Shall I open the window? You look a bit pale?'
   'No. I'm fine. Was that all three?'
   'One more to come.

"If potato pulp
Is the same as you
Then we can't talk
If dead end eggs
Hold all that is
You and me
Then stop
Try it
Who knows?
It never was
It never could be
Nothing happened
As always . . .”

'What do you think?'
   'I'm really sorry, I'll have to go.'
   'Oh right. Were they that bad?'
   'They were challenging. Really, really challenging. Can I ask
a big favour?'
   'Sure.'
   'Could you pay me up front?'
   'For what?'
   'We've had three consultations. That's sixty pounds.'

'If Channel 4 uses them.'

'And I'm unleashing your creative genius.'

'That's true. I don't suppose a poet earns much.'

'No. Have you spoken to the partners about having me in residence?'

'Not yet. The trouble is, you're not very evidence-based.'

'Meaning?'

'There aren't any targets for poetry. So I doubt you're a top priority.'

'Patients would love it.'

'It's not about what patients want. It's about what we get paid for. Is fifty all right for now?'

BARRY

'Dr Phil, can I ask you something personal?'

'Anything you like.'

'I've just watched you go in and out of the staff toilet.'

'Right.'

'And there's no way you were in there long enough to wash your hands afterwards.'

'Oh, I never wash my hands after a pee.'

'What – never?'

'Hardly ever.'

'Why not?'

'Because there's no need. I have a shower once, maybe twice a day and I wash all over, paying special attention to the genital area. Don't you?'

'Of course.'

'So your penis is as clean, if not cleaner, than the rest of your body.'

'So?'

'So you don't run to wash your hands when you touch your elbow or your nose, so why do it when you touch your penis?'

'Surely the point is that you wash after weeing in case you get urine on your hands.'

'When did you last piss on your hands?'

'I can't remember.'

'Even if you've got the shakes, urine is sterile, unless you've got an infection.'

'So it's safe to drink your own urine?'

'In moderation. The first hormone replacement therapy was

made from the urine of pregnant mares and another used the urine of virginal women.'

'Where did they get that then?'

'From a nunnery in France.'

'Assuming that all French nuns are virgins?'

'Well, I expect they do extra checks while they're giving the sample.'

'With a shaving mirror on a stick?'

'Probably.'

'Faeces isn't sterile though, is it?'

'Oh no, it's chock-full of bacteria. Anaerobes, coliforms, enterococci – ten to the power of ten per gram wet weight.'

'That's normal, is it?'

'Yes. They live quite happily in the bowel and serve a useful function in food digestion. You just wouldn't want them in your breakfast or your bloodstream.'

'So presumably you wash your hands after opening your bowels.'

'Only when I'm at home.'

'Explain.'

'At home, I keep the toilet scrupulously clean. Or rather Dr Rose does. I know I won't pick up anything nasty from the loo roll holder, the seat, the toilet handle or the taps. So I can wipe and wash with confidence.'

'But excreting out is different?'

'Oh yes. You never know who's left what where. So you can wash your hands and then immediately desterilise them again with something far more unpleasant on the taps or the door handle.'

'Like what?'

'Well, normal excrement is bad enough but say you go in after a small boy with hepatitis A? Or someone with food poisoning and gastro-enteritis? Salmonella, campylobacter, clostridium, E. coli – you name it, it's been found on the walls of a public toilet. Even the twenty-pee entrance machine's filthy.'

'So what's the solution?'

'Don't go in public. If you must, hover over the bowl, don't wipe or wash, operate all doors with your feet and jump over the turnstile.'

'But you risk soiling your pants.'

'Better that than crippling abdominal pain, diarrhoea and vomiting.'

'What about crabs?'

'What about them?'

'Well, you've seen the graffiti. "There's no use standing on the seat, the crabs in here can jump ten feet."'

'Scaremongering. Crabs cling to hair, so you don't get them from toilets, sheets or towels.'

'That's a relief.'

'But you can get them in your eyebrows.'

'Can you get the clap from a toilet seat?'

'Extremely unlikely.'

'How do you know?'

'American researchers swabbed the toilet seats from seventy-two public restrooms in Oregon and failed to grow any gonorrhoea.'

'That's hardly proof.'

'No, but they also smeared urethral discharge from patients with gonorrhoea onto toilet seats and timed how long the bacteria survived.'

'And?'

'Two hours tops.'

'So I could get it?'

'Theoretically. But sexually transmitted diseases are far more likely to be transmitted sexually. So the only way you're likely to get one from a toilet is . . .'

'. . . If I sit down without realising someone's already on there.'

'Precisely.'

RUBY

'Morning, Ruby. What can I do for you?'

'My husband wants to smell my feet.'

'Is this the same husband who was washing in urine?'

'Yes. Only he seems to have grown out of that now.'

'Socks on or socks off?'

'Does it make a difference?'

'No idea, I'm playing for time until Dr Google answers his bleep.'

'Is it normal?'

'I doubt it. But neither is it likely to be harmful. Has he told you where his motivation is coming from?'

'He says he's locked his sexuality in the closet for too long, and it's time to celebrate his desires, not feel guilty about them.'

'Is he Catholic?'

'Yes.'

'There you are then.'

'But he's lapsed. Now he spends his Sundays at car boot sales.'

'Looking for what?'

'Boots.'

'Very good.'

'Seriously. He buys second-hand boots and takes them up to the box room to sniff them.'

'Anything else?'

'He's taken to masturbating into a sock.'

'Well, we've all done that.'

'I haven't.'

'Most men have. It's usually when you're young and excitable and pumped full of testosterone, and you want to experiment with yourself without leaving telltale snail's tracks on the sheets so your mother won't know.'

'We burned his mother ten years ago.'

'Yes but I'm just saying that using a wank-sock isn't pathological.'

'To save on the laundry bills, maybe not. But he only does it if the sock's really smelly and doesn't belong to him.'

'And how is he generally? His weight? His appetite?'

'Fine.'

'Passing water OK?'

'I don't ask.'

'Bowels regular?'

'Yes. Can I ask where this is leading?'

'NHS broadband is glacially slow. Ah, here's Dr Google now.'

'So you don't know anything about my problem?'

'I'm not even sure if it is a problem. Let's call it a hobby. Do you mind it?'

'Not if it keeps him in the box room. To be honest, we've been getting on each other's nerves a bit since he went semi-retired.'

'What, getting under each other's feet?'

'Are you laughing at me?'

'Sorry. Have you let him anywhere near your feet?'

'Oh yes. I'm very partial to a foot massage and he's always been good at those. But I'm just not sure I want him sniffing them.'

'I bet he's been a closet sniffer for years without you realising. "Hard day at work, love. Feet must be killing you. Kick off those sweaty sandals and let me snort your web spaces."'

'He always insists on kneeling at my feet. I thought it was his eyesight.'

'See? He's been doing it all your married life without you knowing, and now he wants to share his pleasure with you.'

'But why was he hooked on feet in the first place?'

'Who knows? Maybe a maiden aunt used to tickle his feet till he passed out. Maybe his brother used to pin him down, stick dirty socks in his face and say, "Smell the cheese." Or maybe it's because foot sniffing is still a cultural taboo in Britain and he's on a mission to push back the boundaries of sexual experience.'

'But why has he suddenly come out about it? What's given him the courage?'

'Maybe retirement has given him time to reflect on his life.'

'I wouldn't have thought so. Not with the time he spends on that bloody computer.'

'Silver surfer, is he?'

'Yes.'

'Dr Google recommends the Erotic Extremities website. Here we are. "In human sexuality, the most profound taboos are often counterbalanced by intense longings to transgress the fragile borders between the permitted and the forbidden."'

'Oh, that one looks interesting.'

'Champion the Wonder Pony?'

'Yes. I've wanted a pony ever since I was a girl. But we never had the paddock for it.'

'What's your husband's back like?'

'Fine. He's strong as an ox.'

'"Includes American saddle and quality riding whip. Discreet delivery guaranteed in forty-eight hours." Shall I write down the address?'

'If you wouldn't mind, doctor.'

'Go easy on the stirrups.'

ALI

'Hello, Ali.'

'Hi.'

'Are you all right?'

'Sort of. And you?'

'Great. Channel 4 will be out by Friday and the partners want to meet you. Two are for, two against and one undecided.'

'Oh, right. Thanks.'

'Have you got a poem for me?'

'No, a breast lump.'

'Shit. How long have you had it?'

'Relax. That's your sort of humour, right?'

'Not in a consultation. Comedy is context.'

'I thought comedy was unexpected.'

'I'm having a break from it. Trying to be positive and serious. Gloria thinks it will play better.'

'Good. Well, yes, I have got a poem for you.'

'Is it my turn to lie down?'

'Yes please.'

'Do I have to take my shoes off?'

'I won't tell if you won't.'

'Is there a title?'

'"Secret".'

'You're not going to tell me?'

'The title is "Secret". Now close your eyes.

"A secret is not a lie
Until you deny

Its existence
A secret is an untold truth
A silent trust
A shadow, unnoticed
A secret can smoulder like a hot cinder on the
    carpet
It can shake and rattle the bars of its cage
It can dance and tease to be let out
Or it can lie gently wrapped in tissue in the drawer
    of my mind
Like a glass bauble, precious, fragile, mutely
    beautiful

If I am quite alone
I can take it out and hold it to the light
To see all its colours
But if I were to drop it
Or someone else should break it
Then a quiet secret could become an exploding
    bomb
Scattering shattering splinters of glass
In uncontrollable directions
With unintentional searing pain
A protected secret, kept whole
Has a priceless value
And a beauty of its own
A secret is a dancing shadow
A silent trust
A mutual truth.'"

'I don't know what to say.'
    'That's because you rarely take anything seriously.'
    'Is it about me?'
    'It's about whatever you feel it's about.'

'Frank Muir used to say that the secret of character writing is to give people secrets.'

'It's not about Frank Muir. We need to work on your emotional depth.'

'So what is your secret?'

'I'm wasting my life chasing something pointless.'

'Is that a dig?'

'No. But why are you obsessed with television? What's wrong with being just a GP?'

'Nothing. Apart from the fact that my head would explode.'

'One day a week is such a waste of you.'

'I couldn't do it full time. My dad was a workaholic who got depressed and took his life. I don't want to go the same way. I'm pacing myself.'

'So you're not a vain, superficial, untrustworthy self-publicist?'

'Not just that, no. Are you sure you don't have a breast lump?'

'Yes. And I don't want a TUBE either.'

'That's not what I meant.'

'What's your secret?'

'Oh, God. I dunno. When I was a teenager, I nearly burnt down a house by not stubbing out a cigar properly.'

'Oh, you'll have to do better than that, Dr Mitty.'

'Can we turn the tape off?'

NOTE TO GLORIA

Gloria,

Here's the script for my first ever gig at the Venue comedy club in Bristol, December 1989, as a warm-up for Arnold Brown. He was brilliant. Opening line: 'Not too much applause, please. That's how fascism started.'

I used to write out every routine in longhand, as a security blanket. I didn't use all of this, just the bits I could remember. Most of it got an airing at the Edinburgh Fringe with *Struck Off and Die*, a double act with Tony Gardner. We folded after a good review: 'What makes this show rise above mediocre is the genuine comic talent of Tony Gardner.'

The unbroadcastable story at the end was broadcast on Radio 4's *Fringe Fever* in 1990, I think. Could have been 1991. It got huge numbers of complaints, upheld by the Broadcasting Standards Council. Inappropriate material for a comedy show, apparently.

I thought at the time it might be useful for people to appreciate the causes of the emotionally crippled culture they encounter. And it's a historical record of what being a junior doctor in the late eighties did to your mind. Well mine, anyway.

Phil

PS This is definitely not for broadcast.
PPS If you want more HRT, you need to come in and have
your blood pressure checked.

THE WATERSHED
Bristol, December 1989

Hello. I'm Dr Phil.

Yes, I am a real doctor. Don't be alarmed. Just bask in my rainbow of patronisation. I do tend to use medical jargon that may be hard for the lay person to follow. For example, Kenneth Clarke is what we doctors like to call a fat bastard.

Our hospital's got a new sign up: 'Warning. Guard Dogs Operating on this Site'. We've got some bad surgeons but . . .

If junior doctors were prisoners of war, then under the Geneva Convention the sleep deprivation we suffer would be considered torture. In the NHS, it's considered the only way to learn. As my consultant says, 'It never did me any harm.' No, it didn't. You lonely, divorced, alcoholic bigot.

There are 30,000 junior doctors in the UK, and 90,000 counsellors. That's one to kill the patient and three to ask the relatives how they feel.

The great thing about the NHS is there's so much to whinge about. In a bad week, I do 120 hours. The Tories say they want to halve our hours but they won't double our numbers. So there'll be one junior doctor running round like a maniac covering the entire hospital at night. Oh, we have that already. It's called private medicine.

Yep, there's nowhere quite as scary as the private hospital at night. I worked in one – on my own, with the odd nurse in it for the Luncheon Vouchers. Some people had major surgery but there was no intensive care. The cardiac arrest trolley consisted of a bottle of port. And the death certificate book.

If you do go private, I'd suggest the private wing of an NHS hospital so there's an anaesthetist on hand if things go tits up. And never trust a doctor who practises exclusively in the private sector. You've got to be diabolical to get kicked out of the NHS.

There was a senior consultant in London caught trading kidneys. He was picked up by the GMC – yes, they do occasionally do something – and found guilty of serious professional misconduct. His punishment? To work only in the NHS for three years. Christ, it must be bad.

Not sure I'd have my operation in a cottage hospital either; where the bloke who mows the lawn also gives the anaesthetic. And the last time they used a defibrillator was to jump-start the tractor.

Private medicine has one advantage. It teaches consultants to communicate. 'Hello, Mrs Jenkins. Come and grab a seat next to me. You can't see/move? Ah, yes, cataracts/hips. There's a two-year wait, I'm afraid. Of course, you could have it done tomorrow. Yes, really. By me. All you have to do is pay for it. What's a nest egg for if not to give you the wonderful gift of sight/movement?'

Australian doctors love coming here. You can try out stuff in the NHS you'd never be allowed to do at home. Which is why they call us POMs – that's Practise On Me. And then if it all goes pear-shaped, you're back in Perth before the lawyers get the scent.

That's not to say overseas doctors get a good deal here. Especially if they're not – how shall I put this? – Caucasian. They get all the shitty, non-consultant jobs that no one else will do. Think Empire sweatshop.

And there's never anything to eat when you're on call. The reason we draw the curtains around the bed when you've died is so we can raid the fruit bowl without anybody noticing.

That's not strictly true. Hospital curtains never quite go round the bed. There's always that two-foot gap for the voyeur in the bed opposite. Just right for vaginal examinations. And because it's the NHS, there isn't any jelly. You're lucky to get a glove. But you will get some knackered, stubbly house officer, smelling of stale gin, who whacks two fingers in without asking. Then he lines up a dozen medical students to have a go. And if you say no, they'll do it to you anyway under anaesthetic. It's called informed consent.

No wonder people take the risk of going private. A clean bright room to yourself in a converted Georgian mansion, with a jacuzzi, a twenty-four-hour Belgian chef and a view of the rose garden. And you get the top man, the consultant – daytime hours only – and he's all smiley in a pristine suit. And he's got gloves and plenty of jelly and it's all nice and warm. And he slips one finger in ever so gently. And he slips another finger in ever so gently. And then he does that thing with his thumb. 'Would you like side to side, up and down or round and round? Have what you like, dear, you're paying for it.'

How many male gynaecologists does it take to change a light bulb? Just one. And while you're asleep, he'll rip out the socket, the wiring and the fuse board.

Why do relatives bring in hampers of fruit for patients who can't eat? Does it heal by osmosis?

'He can't be dead, doctor, he's eaten all his plums.'

'Yth hi hth, hthn't hi?'

Get your gums around my plums. If I say it in front of 500 people in Bristol, it's a bad gag. If I say it to one of you in the privacy of my consulting room, it's serious professional misconduct. I guess that's safety in numbers. My plums against yours.

So why the long hours? Because we're cheap. Junior doctors are paid for overtime at a third their basic rate. If I work 120 hours a week, for eighty of those I'll get a big, fat £1.70 an hour. That's less than the hippo keeper at Bristol Zoo. For doing much the same job.

If I run to your cardiac arrest in the middle of the night, defibrillate you, save your life and go back to bed, I'll earn around 12 pence. The price of a Fudge finger. The lowest-paid hospital porter earns three times that for picking up the laundry. So when the crash bleep goes, I grab a bag of sheets on the way.

They put 'Not for 222' above the beds on one ward. That means if your heart stops, we don't bother calling the crash team. Might be for a good reason but no one bothers to check with the patients.

'What does that sign mean, doctor?'

'Oh, it's nothing to do with you.'

If a surgical registrar takes out your appendix in the middle of the night, he'll earn less than the price of one stitch. If a consultant who hasn't seen an appendix for thirty years does it privately, he'll charge a thousand times more. That's because the scar will be a thousand times bigger.

My other top tip for a 120-hour week is to combine your bodily functions. I eat, sleep, piss, wank, crap and watch *Neighbours* in the bath. It's called multi-skilling. And it leaves me plenty of time to enjoy my hobby. Cleaning the bath.

And why is it that doctors never get chocolates but nurses always do? Is it because they care? I did a house job at Frenchay Hospital and three student nurses rewrote 'Merry Christmas, Ev'rybody' for the hospital show. The chorus went:

> So here it is, geriatrics
> Ev'rybody's had a stroke
> Let's get the turkey out
> And see how many choke . . .

There's no excuse for that sort of humour. Nurses only have to do eight-hour shifts with guaranteed fag breaks. I have to work an eighty-hour shift, 9 a.m. Friday to 5 p.m. Monday. So how do I survive? Simple. Steal the nurses' chocolates. Students usually fall for the old 'look up there' while you grab a handful of Roses. Staff nurses look away if you flood the kitchen. But it takes a machete-wielding maniac to get Night Sister away from the Milk Tray. Look. Her hand's still in the box.

You won't see that on *Casualty*. Sister Duffy and her happy band of carers. If someone's found dead on the toilet in Holby, the whole cast's in tears. If that happened in a real casualty department, they'd all be pissing themselves. Sister'd be in there like a shot, silly hat on, take a Polaroid, stick it on the noticeboard and laugh at it for months.

Yes, I'm afraid NHS staff do occasionally let the professionalism slip and laugh at patients. I worked for a gynaecologist who admitted an extraordinarily large woman for a womb scrape. But when he got her on the table, he just couldn't reach. So he wrote back to the GP: 'I am unable to perform this procedure without the aid of a miners' lamp and a canary.' In Taunton, cerebrally challenged patients are NFB, or Normal For Bridgewater. In Winchester, it's NFA, Normal for Andover. In Norfolk, it's NFN, Normal for Norfolk – must be a tough place to work. Birmingham is NFR, Normal for Redditch, but NFR also stands for Not for Resuscitation, so you have to be careful.

In casualty, patients are either PAFO – Pissed and Fell Over, PAGOT – Pissed and Got Thumped, or PADEE – Pissed and Denies Everything. On the Isle of Wight, fat patients are DTS – Danger to Shipping. Patients on their way out are either JPFROG – Just Plain Fucking Run Outta Gas – or TSBUNDY – Totally Stuffed But Unfortunately Not Dead Yet.

Back in 1978 a pseudonymous American doctor called Samuel Shem coined the acronym GOMER – Get Out of My Emergency Room – in his book, *The House of God*.

GOMERS are human beings who have lost what goes

into being human beings. They want to die, and we will not let them. We're cruel to the Gomers, by saving them, and they're cruel to us, by fighting tooth and nail against our trying to save them. They hurt us, we hurt them.

His solution was to pass the buck on to other departments by a process called turfing. Shem described how raising the bed to five feet allows a Gomer to fall and fracture a hip ('TURF TO ORTHOPAEDICS') and at six feet, a fall results in a head injury ('TURF TO NEUROSURGERY'). The NHS is full of patients who demonstrate the sheer futility of struggling on past their sell-by date. They get labelled crud or crumble, bed-blockers or social admissions. The relatives don't want to know and the staff survive on black humour.

Here's a GOMER rating scale for elderly patients a friend of mine found pinned up in a Liverpool casualty department. Doctors compete with each other to see whose patient gets the most points.

Admitting letter from GP ends with 'sorry'	10 points
Hideous relatives insist something must be done	15 points
Toenails cannot be cut with nail clippers	20 points
Answers 'yes' to all questions	30 points
Answers 'yes' to all questions asked to other patients in the room	40 points
Answers 'yes' when not asked any questions at all	50 points
Easier to understand without dentures	75 points
Unrequested stool specimen found. Ten feet from bed	100 points
Faecal impaction under fingernails	200 points

Call me old-fashioned but I don't want to spend the end of my days shitting in the corridor and being the butt of a casualty officer's joke. Pass me the pillow, please.

The most outrageous thing about being a doctor is not the humour but the lack of accountability. If you're really bad, they reward you for it. If you kill a patient or you shag a patient, they suspend you on full pay. Shag a patient to death and they suspend you on double pay. It's performance-related.

OK, I'm exaggerating. You don't get suspended for shagging a patient. Only if you're caught. Which means either the lock on the mortuary door doesn't work, or the patient comes out of the anaesthetic a bit too early.

Nurses, on the other hand, can be sacked for eating a patient's pudding. And they have to wear those ridiculous hats like cake decorations and highly flammable uniforms made out of J-cloths. No wonder they're so grumpy.

Some academics have called for a merger of medical and nursing training, so we could iron out prejudices and learn from each other's roles. It'd be a disaster. We'd end up with nurses who drink ten pints, drop their trousers and piss in people's flower beds. And doctors would have to go on a three-week course to get a shiny badge before they can so much as fart on the ward.

I've decided to get away from this madness and to give up medicine. I'm training to be a GP. Ken Clarke has accused us of reaching for our wallets. Bollocks. Have you seen the cost of a tweed jacket with real leather elbow patches? And Nature Treks aren't cheap either. A rural GP's been in the news because he couldn't get an ambulance in the middle of the night for a critically ill patient. So he put a drip up, stuck her in the back of his Land Rover and drove her all the way to hospital. Now that's dedication. Then he ruined it by asking for some petrol money. 'Thirsty beasts, those four-by-fours.'

Ken's NHS is all about sticking to budgets. GPs aren't going to want sick patients with expensive drugs on their lists. The trick is to build your health centre on a big hill, so only the healthy make it to the top. And if they do make it past the bearded receptionist, have really low bucket seats in the waiting room that no one over forty can get out of.

In general practice, most patients are TATT – Tired All the Time – and end up with TEETH – Tried Everything Else, Try Homeopathy. And the waiting rooms are full of OHSIMCWHELA. That's Otherwise Healthy Semi-Intellectual Middle-Class Worriers with High Expectations and Low Achievements. They're tired and depressed. But life failure isn't a diagnosis. So it's probably a virus.

The trouble with labels is that once you've got one, you can't shake it off. A friend of mine works in endocrinology and spends Tuesdays down at the FHWC – Fat Hairy Woman Clinic. One of his patients, 'a larger than average woman with a downy covering', was found to have a benign tumour in her pituitary gland. This tumour would have remained there for keeps with no life-threatening consequences but was almost certainly causing her appearance by excreting more masculinising chemicals than strictly necessary.

The staff presumed that she would like to have it treated and urged her to have something radioactive beamed up her nostrils to destroy it. Hey presto, she returned to the clinic three months after treatment slim and hair-free. And single. Her husband, it appears, fancied her precisely because she was fat and hairy. He left her for a woman he met in the clinic. She was incurable.

Most patients don't want us to change them. They just want us to make them well enough to do the things that made them sick in the first place. But the politicians just won't accept it. We always have to change everything and everyone; tell the poor people how to behave.

Ken tries to justify his health service reforms by saying he has medical advisers. That means he's hand-picked a few doctors even more right wing than he is to tell him what he already thinks. Ken smokes. His adviser Lord Trafford smoked so much he died of lung cancer. Ken believes that health ministers have the right to choose bad habits but then bribes GPs to coerce women into having cervical smears. Doctors aren't government enforcers. We can point out risks but we can't force you to have a smear. It's called rape.

Another of Ken's gems is for GPs to herd up everyone over seventy-five, measure them, weigh them, check their blood pressure and test their urine. Why? There's no evidence it'll do any good. Anyone over seventy-five who isn't already known to their doctor is either extremely healthy or doesn't want a doctor anywhere near them. And quite right, too. You're just having a tug to *Dynasty* and there's a gingernut GP passing a urine pot through your letter box.

Medical school is bollocks too. Instead of telling you how to explain to someone why his leg needs amputating, they teach you about the physiology of the chick biventer cervicis muscle. The rest of your time is centred around shit. We used to play a game called freckle. You sit around the table with your chums and deal a pack of cards. First person to get an ace has to do a turd on the table. The next has to take his shoe off and hit the turd as hard as he can. The person who ends up with the most freckles has to buy the next round. How do you think I got these? Cheers.

And let's not forget bladder tennis. Spilt into pairs, catheterise each other, join them up and pee into each other's bladders. 'Fifteen–love!' Glory days.

Then up to the wards to play doctors. The great thing about wearing a white coat is that you can stick your finger up someone's arse within a minute of meeting them. And they'll be grateful. A bit like being in the Young Conservatives.

To be fair, I'm more holistic than that. Occasionally I'll wander up to the head end and explain what I'm doing. Not that it does any good. I gained informed consent from a senior lady recently and popped my finger in the rectum. She lifted her head off the pillow and said, 'Is that you, George?'

A friend of mine did a home visit on an old lady who was 'off her legs'. He carried her up the stairs, examined her very thoroughly – front and back – dressed her and carried her back down the stairs. She said, 'Are you the doctor?'

The first day at medical school is dissection, so the first patient you meet is a dead one. Start as you mean to go on. No one prepares you for the stench of formalin or the sound of the jig saw slicing off the top of the skull. Or the sight of the unfeasibly large genitals swollen in the preservation process. A few girlies faint but by the end of the first week, we're all making penis key rings, skipping with the intestines and playing 'one hand one knee' with the heart.

Our professor of anatomy took us around a cadaver on our first day. 'There are just two things you need to learn to survive in medicine. The first is to be disgusted by nothing.' So he sticks his finger up the corpse's arse then puts it in his mouth. 'Now your turn.' We didn't want to but you don't like to upset him – he's the professor; you might need a reference. So we all followed suit. As I recall it was more chemically than shitty but I may have just blotted it out. Then he said, 'The second thing you need to survive in medicine is observation: I put my *index* finger in the arse and my *middle* finger in my mouth.'

The bastard. We were all sick, for about half an hour, and then the penny dropped. This was our initiation ceremony, our rite of passage. 'Bloody funny – only way to learn.'

So I should have been ready for the professor of pathology:

'Come over here, Hammond. There's a woman with a clitoris like a gherkin.'

'That big?'

'No, that bitter.'

I am available for children's parties.

231

If you survive medical school with your empathy intact, it soon gets beaten out of you as a junior doctor. At the back end of an eighty-hour shift, the only way to cope is not to care. You're so knackered you celebrate when patients die on the way to hospital because you don't have to get out of bed to treat them. It doesn't say that in the Hippocratic oath.

The health service is run by Fat Ken, a man with no medical expertise, who divides his time between Rushcliffe, Ronnie Scott's and a small office in the Department of Health, where he tries to control a workforce of a million people in between cigarillos and real ale. And we wonder why the NHS is in the shit.

Fortunately Ken has an army of NHS managers, who failed to get on in supermarkets and have no idea what it's like on the front line. Their brief is simple: stick to the budget and avoid a major political scandal. Pay the staff a pittance and then frighten them into silence. Job contracts now contain gagging clauses, forbidding staff to speak to the press, even if lives are in danger. A family planning doctor in Bath was suspended for speaking out about cuts in the service. Staff won't even criticise the lentil lasagne in the hospital canteen. The NHS is run on fear. Fuck 'em all. They don't know where I live . . . Oh, you do? We'd better cut that bit out then.

Fat Ken has just regraded all the nurses. Midwives are particularly pleased. To be a midwife you have to be a staff nurse first, do another eighteen months' training, pass exams, deal with pushy NCT parents, absent anaesthetists, dangerous junior doctors, male obstetricians, miscarriages, stillbirths, abnormal babies and the constant threat of litigation. And for all this, you get paid a thousand pounds less than when you started. Complain and you'll be sacked. Just don't take it out on the babies.

It was much more fun in Jersey. There's no NHS there, beer is 20p a pint and even specky, freckly, ginger people can get a shag. If they've got a white coat. I worked on the coronary care unit where every bed had its own TV. In the NHS, you're lucky to get a pillow. The theory was that recovering from a heart attack is much less stressful if you can keep abreast of the soaps. The practice is that you end up shocking to *Top of the Pops*. 'The only way is up . . .'

A casualty officer I know was on duty at Westminster Hospital in 1984 – something of a rarity under normal circumstances – but word had come in that Tommy Cooper had collapsed during the recording on *Live at Her Majesty's* and was being rushed in. There was a big reception committee. Even a few consultants got out of bed. Tommy looked dead on arrival but they went through the motions, cutting off his jacket as doves, packs of cards and knotted silk hankies flew everywhere. The poor casualty officer had to get a drip into a vein, in full view of a dozen senior colleagues. It took him two goes, forgivable if he hadn't said, 'Shit! Not like that – like *that*.' Nobody laughed. His best gag ever and nobody laughed. Tommy Cooper would have laughed.

Diagnosing death is tricky, especially in very large patients. They've got so much padding that it's hard to feel a pulse or hear the lungs. In Jersey, a student nurse stumbled on a large man having a mid-afternoon nap, thought he'd died, taped his eyelids down and covered him in daffodils. He was very distressed when he woke up.

A friend of mine was called to the ward to see another large non-mover. He couldn't find a pulse, so he certified him dead and told the nurses to call the relatives. When they arrived, he was sitting up in bed and reading the *Sun*. So technically he was still dead. But when he started tucking into lunch, they demanded an explanation. My mate Dr Phil – no relation – could have just blamed it on the nurses. But instead he leant forward earnestly and said, 'The thing is, there are different stages of death.' Don't doctors talk bollocks when we have to?

And when we're not talking bollocks, we talk euphemisms: 'There may be a bit of a wait' means 'We take Visa'.

'Your mother's taken a turn for the worse' means that she died three hours ago and we've only just noticed. So while you're rushing in to hospital, she's lying there colder than a polar bear's knob. So the nurses pop her in a piping-hot bath to warm her up a bit. Then they prop her up in bed with a hot-water bottle, oxygen mask and headphones on, listening to hospital radio, and the moment you hit the ward: 'Oh, you've just missed her. She's peaceful now.'

By the time I get to the body, the nurses have nicked the watch. Can you blame them? Going home every night with shit under your fingernails to your little cell in the nurses' home. And every box is the same, six foot by three foot, with a mug stand, a mobile, a spider plant ('They're so hard to kill'), a big fluffy duvet, a Garfield poster with the top right-hand corner coming away to reveal a blob of Blu-tack and a half-empty bottle of White Musk from the Body Shop next to the cotton buds, the Canesten and the pile of watches.

The flu only seems to affect nurses, not doctors. The reason's obvious: doctors don't touch patients unless they absolutely have to. That doesn't mean I'm entirely pro-nurse. They do have a sick leave book that fills up suspiciously far in advance. But you can't doubt their intellect. I was at a cardiac arrest and the student nurse said, 'Don't worry, Mr Saunders, your heart's stopped but we're trying to get it started.' There wouldn't even have been a cardiac arrest if she hadn't turned off the flashing box because it was disturbing everyone's sleep.

Another friend of mine was assisting a surgeon who was trying to remove an appendix through the smallest hole possible. My friend had been out for a few beers and a curry the night before, and as he pulled on the retractor, his bowels got the better of him. He unleashed a silent-but-deadly. The registrar said, 'I smell faeces.' The consultant went, 'I smell faeces too. Damn! I must have perforated the bowel. We'll have to open him up.'

Bit of an ethical dilemma here. Should my friend own up and say, 'I made that heinous smell in your pristine operating theatre. Can I have my reference now, please?' Or should he keep mum and watch this poor sod zipped open while they search for a non-existent hole in his bowel? But my friend – Dr Phil, no relation – was brighter than that. He leant forward and whispered to his boss, 'I think it was Sister.' If in doubt, blame it on the nurses.

Which is a bit tough, because nurses are the only ones who teach you anything. Training is by the miracle of osmosis. See one, do one, teach one and fly by the seat of your pants. I remember my first liver biopsy. I had seen one before – on *Casualty* – so off I went, kit under one arm and *Procedures in Practice* under the other. Unpacked the kit. The needle was huge. Never mind; page 13, here we go. I got a bit of liver . . . a bit of kidney, a bit of thyroid, a bit of spleen. It was more of a kebab, really. But the patient was effusively grateful. Bought me a bottle of whisky. People you nearly kill thank you. People you save sue you. What's all that about then?

Generally, the British are too trusting. You could put a Rottweiler in a white coat and kick it on to the wards, all the patients would go, 'Oh, he's a lovely doctor, that one. Ever so friendly, great big paws, comes up and licks your face. Don't like the way he cocks his leg on my barley sugars though. Still, they gotta learn.'

At least dogs are good communicators. Very good at unconditional love. Doctors aren't. Nobody teaches us how to talk to patients. I know an arsehole obstetrician – that's not a job, it's a description – who says to any woman who claims their pregnancy was an accident, 'Don't tell me – you were walking down the high street, fell over a loose paving slab and fell on to an erect penis.' But the worst consultation I've witnessed was a busy gynaecology clinic with a registrar who didn't have time to read the notes properly: 'Hello, have a seat. You'll be pleased to know you don't have cervical cancer . . . Oh! Yes you do.'

Doctors aren't selected for our human qualities. We've all got three grade-A science A-levels and the communication skills of a dead skunk. Throw in five years of freckle and eighty hours on call without food or sleep, and you wonder why we aren't more caring. But thanks to a fantastic new book, *Surgical Diagnosis and Management* by Dunn and Rawlinson, we now know how to break bad news. I know what you're thinking: learning how to break bad news from a surgeon's like being taught how to fly by a pastry chef. But it's the only thing we've got. Page 121: 'Informing the relatives of a patient who has died. One. Explain that the patient died peacefully and was not in any pain.' Nice sentiment. But most of us die with a junior doctor jumping up and down on our chest: 'Where have you hidden the chocolates?'

'Two. Where appropriate, physical contact can do more good than ten minutes' talking.' 'G'day. I've killed your mum. Would you like a hug?'

'Three. It is a help to ask for a senior nurse to come in and arrange for refreshments to be brought.' 'Ah, Sister, thank God you've arrived. That's one, two, three choc ices, two raspberry Mivis and a packet of scampi fries.'

Breaking bad news is an art form. I have my hair cut at uneven lengths by a Polish barber on the Gloucester Road to give the impression I've been up all night. And I always wear a pair of warm, empathic, tortoiseshell spectacle frames. Without them I look like a killer. With them I look like I've tried my best. And relatives are less likely to punch you if you're wearing glasses.

The voice is important too. I favour the forced sincerity of Ronald Reagan: 'She's peaceful now.' Stoop slightly, bow your head with reverence, quiver your top lip like a gerbil anticipating a celery stick, as if you're on the verge of tears. When you're starving, sleep-deprived and surrounded by loud wailing, it's surprisingly easy to laugh. Don't. They'll never understand it in court. Always carry an emergency Minto and bite into it if the giggles kick in. Store it under your lower lip in between bites – you're less likely to be attacked if you've got a speech impediment.

Don't, under any circumstances, let the Minto slip around to the side of your cheek. It looks like you're suggesting oral sex. And don't lean over too much – you don't want those bananas falling on the carpet. Above all, don't forget the ash cash. If you can persuade the relatives to opt for a cremation, you'll pocket a tidy £23.50 for filling in the cremation form. If they opt for a formal burial, you get nothing. Remember, you can't bury cancer. You've got to burn it.

The junior doctors in Torbay have clubbed all their ash cash together and bought a boat called the Grim Reaper. Now that's what I call teamwork. I was going to visit until they told me their mess parties are known as the Wart Exchange. Saw enough of those in Jersey. Imported by Nottingham medical students, apparently.

One of the toughest parts of being a doctor is answering difficult questions. Like 'Have you seen my bananas?' or 'Why did he die?' As any pathologist will tell you, doctors get the cause of death wrong at least half the time. And emergency medicine is so complicated. Any patient lucky enough to get a blue-light ambulance screams through the streets at ninety miles an hour, only to sit in casualty for six hours before anybody notices him. The first test we do is called the pumpkin test. We shine a pen torch in your mouth and if your whole head lights up, you're pumpkin-positive. You're headed for the surgical ward and almost certain death.

Most people sign a consent form without bothering to read

it: 'I also consent to any further procedure that is deemed to be necessary at the time. No assurance has been given to me as to which medical practitioner will perform my operation.' It's a licence to kill. Legions of pumpkin-positives are used as midnight cannon fodder for unsupervised surgical trainees. I wish I was joking. But trainee surgeons are left alone to do major surgery for the first time, unsupervised, unfed and unrested, with their consultants not even in the hospital. If it wasn't for the nurses, we'd never hide the carnage.

But before you get a whiff of scalpel, you have to survive the diamorphine stress test. Diamorphine is a fancy name for heroin. We use it by the bucketload to relieve pain and distress. Unfortunately it also relieves respiration, especially if you whack it in too quickly. A friend of mine did just that, and his elderly patient stopped breathing. Fortunately there's an antidote, naloxone. Unfortunately the nurse misheard him and gave him Lanoxin. Three ampoules later and he'd stopped her heart as well as her lungs. Burn the notes, bury the X-rays and laugh it off in the mess.

I notice a few people have walked out tonight. It *is* very hot in here. And medical humour is an acquired bad taste. Can you be a good doctor and have a sick sense of humour? I dunno. Can you survive as a junior doctor without one? I've seen doctors cry with laughter at cardiac arrests. I'm not sure why; it's usually over very quickly. First to the grapes wins. Why is it funny? I suppose it depends what side of the defibrillator you're on. Comedy and tragedy are never far apart. Henri Bergson reckons laughter requires a temporary anaesthesia of the heart. So does a cardiac arrest.

My last hospital job before escaping to general practice is obstetrics and gynaecology. I hate it. It's not the hours or the midwives, it's just I'm not very good at it. I want to be a GP because I can bullshit for England but I'm crap with my hands. When I was a fourth-year medical student, I did a locum on the renal unit at St Thomas's. I didn't really want to but I fancied the girlfriend of the doctor who asked me, and when you've got ginger hair, you'll clutch any straw.

I clearly wasn't safe to be out on my own and I'd never been taught to put in a drip before but I was called to resite one at three o'clock in the morning. Hardly something to get the consultant out of bed for, so I bumbled through and, in my nervousness, flushed it through with an ampoule of potassium chloride rather than saline. The ampoules were identical, the light was dim, I was tired . . . you know how it is. I should have killed her but I was so crap, the drip wasn't in properly and the patient just got searing pain in her arm rather than asystole. I realised my error and lied: 'You must be allergic to saline.'

I left medical school with a fine reference: 'Refuses to take medicine seriously. Does not deserve a St Thomas's house job.' Fair enough. But I still got jobs in Bristol and Bath. As a house officer, I stopped a few patients from breathing by squirting drugs in too quickly but, with the nurses' help, we managed to bring them round.

Somehow I got on the Bath GP training scheme, a fifty-to-one shot. I think I want to be a GP. Or at least I know I can't be a hospital doctor. So what's the first job they give me? Working on a special care baby unit. If you had to design a job that was more inappropriate for me, you couldn't do better than sticking needles, drips and drains into babies that are bright blue and about the size of a kumquat.

The nurses realised I was dangerous, so we did a role reversal. I'd make the tea, they'd put in all the drips and drains and tubes and catheters. They weren't allowed to, so I took the credit. I was allowed to take blood but even that defeated me. Trying to get a needle into a vein in the back of a tiny hand that's pulling away from you with all its might so you can collect a few drops of precious blood. And you've got to do fifteen in a row before breakfast when you've been up all night.

I thought about taking my own blood and filling all the tubes up with that. Sister thought I might be struck off.

SCBU is next to the delivery ward and theatres. If a baby comes out flat as a pancake, you get called. There's no sister to guide you there. Babies' brains need oxygen very quickly. Every second counts. It's no place for Dr Ten Thumbs fumbling through intubation. Jesus, that job was hard. But I didn't let on. You never drop the mask of relaxed brilliance.

I really didn't want to do obstetrics. My first delivery, as a medical student, scarred me for life. The midwife popped out for a fag, I was on my own and the baby's head just appeared with the cord wrapped round it. Never been taught what to do, so I guessed. I put two clamps on, cut the cord and out shot the baby, probably faster than it should have done. The good news? I caught it. The bad news? As well as clamping the cord, I'd clamped two huge great tufts of pubic hair. I didn't want to reclamp in case of bleeding. I cut underneath, leaving two bald tramlines, up and down. So I got my comb out. Gave it the old Bobby Charlton crossover. Waste of time.

I vowed never to do obstetrics again but it's part of my rotation so I have to. In Bath, the midwives do all the simple down-below repairs after childbirth but if it's a major rip they'll bleep Dr Ten Thumbs. Who's never done one before. I'm a bloke and we have trouble visualising the anatomy down there at the best of times. We need a road map and a couple of flags. But on one occasion, it looked like a grenade had gone off. It was swollen and bloody and there were piles like the Hanging Gardens of Babylon. No place for a dabbler. 'Thought of a name yet?'

I had a go, because that's what's expected of you before you ask for help. I tried to think in three dimensions, I tried to oppose the edges – inside of vagina goes to outside of anus – and I put in about three and a half miles of catgut. Positive points first: there was still a hole. Constructive criticisms: there were now two flaps on one side, and only one on the other. I'm no expert but that's not how it looked in the textbook.

What to do? I toyed with just snipping it off but decided that wasn't particularly ethical. She might never pee or have sex again. So I asked for help. The on-call registrar was Bruce, great with hands but unfortunately Australian. He took one look at my handiwork and shouted, 'Fuck me, looks like the mice have been at this!' Thanks a lot, mate. Bruce unpicked Mickey Mouse's picnic and resewed beautifully, pausing only to ask the husband, 'How tight would you like her?'

But even worse than episiotomies is coping with stillbirths. You're given no training or debriefing. Apart from this. You are my therapy session. Sorry. We used to have a bit of group therapy when I worked on special care. A psychologist would sit up one end, crying with all the nurses, while all the doctors sat at the other, emotional cripples staring into their M&S sandwiches. I can cry when a baby dies, if it looks like a baby. But I can't quite relate to the babies that don't look at all like babies.

The worst thing about a stillbirth is that the baby doesn't cry. If you eavesdropped on the birth itself, it seems quite normal. Encouraging midwives telling Mum to push. Expectant Dad resolutely up the head end. To go through all the pain of labour and not hear a cry at the end must be the pits. You still ask what sex it is.

Mind you, hearing a cry when it's supposed to be dead isn't always a blessing. I know a senior midwife who's still in therapy because a late-aborted baby she delivered thirty years ago started to breathe. She was on her own, didn't know what to do; there was nobody to ask. So she put it in the fridge.

If a dead baby looks normal, it's easier to hug but I guess the heartbreak is more. If the baby is very abnormal, the staff have to decide if he or she can somehow be dressed in a way that would make a photo seem like a precious keepsake, rather than a monstrous reminder. So we put baby in a little smock and put a little bonnet on that the nice ladies in the League of Friends shop knit. We aren't undertakers – we have no expertise in embalming; there are no guidelines. I just do it to keep the nurses company. And to reflect on God's great purpose.

One baby looked awful but we thought we could just about get a photo. We were deciding whether he looked better against the dark blue of Sister's uniform or the light blue of the staff nurse's but his head kept flopping forward and all we got was the top of the bonnet. Sister lifted the head back a bit further and as the flash went off, the head flopped forward and fell off on to the floor. Silence. Then I saw Sister's shoulders shaking. She was first to crack. We fell like dominoes. How sick is that? I guess you had to be there. Sticks and stones can break your bones but the NHS breaks your head. I'm off to top myself. I would do, only I'm on call tomorrow.

Goodnight.

GLORIA

'How am I doing?'

'The consultations are a bit of a mixed bag, entertaining in parts. You were right about your early stand-up. Unusable. Have you ever been a psychiatric inpatient?'

'Not yet. But I've written some more poems.'

'Ah, yes. The healing power of art. They show you in a very interesting light. But I think we've got enough now.'

'So what are my chances?'

'I'm not sure *Oprah*'s Dr Phil has much to worry about.'

'Is he way out in front?'

'I've no idea. But at least he hasn't had controlled drugs stolen during his consultations.'

'What's Dr Hilary done now?'

'You still don't get it? The batty woman who reads you poems cleared out your emergency bag while you were lying on the couch with your eyes closed.'

'Ali?'

'She's an addict. Heroin and crack, I think.'

'But her poems were great.'

'I doubt they were hers. The style seemed very uneven. And she'll do anything for a fix.'

'How do you know?'

'She offered to expose you. For money. She'd got through your gear and was desperate.'

'I gave her fifty pounds.'

'Yes, that helped for a few days.'

'So you shopped her?'

'Not immediately. It's a great story.'

'Which we can bury with all the other bad consultations?'

'We could but Channel 4 love it. "Dopey TV doc gives crack addict run of the surgery while meditating to poetry."'

'You can't do that.'

'Shit happens. And it shows you letting patients define their own treatment needs very nicely. Very "new" Labour. Did you not realise your drugs were missing?'

'I haven't checked the bag for ages. I try to get out of visits, they're really time consuming. I don't even know what drugs are in there.'

'None, since you left it unlocked . . .'

'I can never remember the combination.'

'. . . and poking out from under the couch.'

'Where is she now?'

'Holland, I think. With your prescription pad. The police are tracking her but we've got her interview in the can.'

'Jesus.'

'She did say you're the best doctor she's ever had. Wasted on television.'

'You can't use any of it without my consent. I'm withdrawing from the competition.'

'I wouldn't. You'll still get the *Countdown* vote. They're very loyal. Plus a small sympathy-comedy vote. It could raise your profile enough for local radio.'

'Great.'

'And look what happened to Richard Bacon.'

'He took drugs; I only gave mine away.'

'You told Vicky.'

'Who's Vicky?'

'Ali. You told her a secret. Something about trying out diamorphine when you were a junior doctor? You'd drawn it up to give a terminally ill patient but she was dead when you got there, so instead of wasting it, you thought you'd see what it was like. Ring any bells?'

'No.'

'It all got very heavy. You said it helped ease the dead-baby pain?'

'No, I didn't. That was never on tape.'

'We've got it on film.'

'You wired Ali?'

'Yes. We needed to make the story stack up. You look very cute on the couch. Odd socks too. But the fisheye lens is a bitch for double chins. And we never sorted out your nose hair. You shouldn't leave your prescription pad.in an unlocked drawer.'

'That's on film too?'

'Yes. One pad, half a bottle of vodka and thirty-seven signed photos of Des O'Connor.'

'You can't have those. They're for cancer patients only.'

'Sorry, but you know how it works.'

'Is there anything else I can do for you?'

'Just my HRT, please, Dr Phil. Oh, and while I'm here, would you like to be a contestant on *Make Me Gay*?'

EPILOGUE

The World's Greatest TV Doctor was won by *Oprah*'s Dr Phil. *Countdown*'s Dr Phil came joint 87th, just behind Dr Hilary. Dr Raj (34th) got a special commendation for sharing his work with his colleagues. 'Dr' Gillian took an ambitious lead but was forced into early retirement by Dr Ben's dead cat. The highest-placed UK entrant was Lord Bob (17th).

Dr Phil can be contacted at drphil@bbc.co.uk and booked to open pharmacy extensions via Vivienne Clore at vclore@richstonepart.co.uk. He can be heard live on BBC Radio Bristol (94.9FM) between 10 a.m. and 1 p.m. on Saturdays. You can listen any time at www.bbc.co.uk/bristol/local_radio/ – it's the place to be, apparently.

Dr Phil presents *The Music Group* on BBC Radio 4. He writes for *Private Eye* and the *Mendip Times*, celebrating life on the Mendips and in surrounding areas. He still appears on *Countdown* but rather spoiled his last outing on *Have I Got News For You* by trying to win. He is hoping to get his own TV series soon. In the meantime, he is Alan Partridge.

Dr Phil is not currently available for consultations pending an inquiry by the General Medical Council. He is 128,944th in the queue but the complaint is important to them. A judgment on Dr Crippen is expected imminently.

'Hippo Crates' was written by Aidan Healy. Other poems are from *Pastries for the Dyslexic* by Frozen Cheesecake (unpublished).

Dr Rose is still lovely – and very patient.
www.drphil2.com